For Maria, as always

# CONTENTS

# ACKNOWLEDGEMENTS

I would like to thank the following people who have had various roles in making this book a reality, particularly Dan Franklin, my editor for more than thirty years, and Patrick Walsh, as well as his assistant at the PEW Agency, John Ash. My friend the artist Jonny Gibbs produced the superb cover and wonderful woodcut images, as he has for four of my previous books. It is always a pleasure and privilege to work with him. Daisy Watt steered the book through the editing and proof stages with great courtesy and efficiency. These five are the team that has shaped and supported the book's preparation.

My neighbours John and Ruth Everett made one piece in the book possible. My friends Tim Dee, Patrick Barkham, Peter Marren, David Tipling and my brother Andy Cocker were companions on several excursions that yielded various parts of the book. My main debt goes to my wife Mary and also to our daughters, Rachael and Miriam, who are often implied by the use of the first-person plural in some of the stories. Without their unacknowledged companionship the writing would have been mere work.

Finally I am deeply grateful to Archant and Guardian newspapers for the opportunities to write on my favourite subjects and then for permission to produce my articles in book form.

# INTRODUCTION

Over the last ten years I have taught nature writing as part of my freelance work. Two of the most memorable and instructive of these experiences have been at Lumb Bank of the Arvon Foundation. The mill-owner's house has a dramatic hilltop location near the village of Heptonstall, just west of Halifax, and was once the home of Ted Hughes. My weeks there were notable mainly because of the company and talents of my respective co-tutors, the innovative writer and activist Paul Kingsnorth and the equally gifted Scottish poet Kathleen Jamie.

I recall vividly an occasion when Paul, in a preamble about his approach to writing on nature, declared that, much as we might admire the work of the eighteenth-century cleric Gilbert White, it is no longer possible for us to think and write as White had once done. Too much anthropogenic water had flowed under nature's bridge since the eighteenth century for us to take the same simple descriptive approach. Life in all its parts is too assailed, too fragile, too precariously placed for us to sustain the good vicar's quasi-scientific detachment. What was required now of an author on nature was a completely updated and upgraded moral perspective. On hearing his entirely reasonable argument I remember thinking to myself, 'Oh dear!' It was both troubling and inwardly amusing, because it occurred to me that White's approach was pretty much exactly what I am still doing. Strike one against me.

On another occasion a year later I was listening to Kathleen Jamie outline her own sense of what was needed for modern nature writing. Precise and accurate descriptions of the other parts of life were important and necessary, she suggested. Yet were they, by themselves, really enough? Her inclination was to say 'no'. What supplies the keystone in any arc of words between an author and their subject and then the all-important reader is some connective story, some fabric of human emotion, that gives the other parts of life their context and rationale. Once again, I gulped inwardly. Descriptive passages that are almost free from any sense of human story are often all that I aspire to. Strike two!

Both of them are, of course, absolutely right. The best nature writing has to contain some narrative thread that acts as the key underpinning motive for the reader's engagement. Nor, today, can it be rapture or curiosity alone, given the fact that the *State of Nature* report in 2016 judged England to be the twenty-eighth most denatured country on Earth; and that the World Wide Fund for Nature's Living Planet Report of 2014 indicated that 52 per cent of all the world's wildlife populations have been lost in the last forty years, during which period our own human numbers have doubled. What place, then, for a book like this one?

It is, in many ways, a modest project. Like its earlier sister volume *Claxton: Field Notes from a Small Planet*, it is a collection of essays, often previously published in the *Guardian* as part of my contributions to the newspaper's venerable 'Country Diary' column. They are arranged chronologically, with the day of the month privileged before the year, so that in any of the twelve chapters an article from 2018 may appear before one from 2012. The intentions are to recreate a single-year cycle and to bring to the fore an unfolding sense of seasonal change and of the minutiae present in one English parish – that of Claxton in Norfolk – where we have lived for the last eighteen years.

This allows me to impart, perhaps merely subliminally, a central message of my own about the natural world and the author's role in relation to it: that the business of transcribing nature and wildlife, of remodelling them through the imagination, is by itself an honourable goal. Because something positive and unexpected occurs in that simple act of recollection. An unannounced element creeps into this accounting. Naming the parts of life becomes, at its best, a record of intimacy. And the more detail that is captured, the more feeling that can be recovered. A crucial part of the exercise is that it taps into and evokes for the reader their own submerged experiences of similar places or encounters, restoring what is often only half-remembered, but indisputably precious and important.

Readers have noticed, and sometimes complained, about the previous volume – and will find in this one – that there is an element of repetition. Or rather, I should say, that they will find the same theme tackled more than once. I make no apology for it but I should perhaps explain its purpose. Our society is sometimes too fixated with relentless novelty to appreciate that much of life is a routine. We derive most from it when we learn how to revisit the same experience again and again, but with renewed sensitivity. No one will benefit from yoga by doing it once. Its meaning lies precisely in the repetition. It is the same with nature. No meeting with a flower, or animal, or place, is ever the same as the last. I have tried to capture these nuances, these minute differences of inner emotion or outer physical detail, for this is the foundation of a full relationship. If *Claxton* and *A Claxton Diary* are anything, they are an expression of this aspiration.

There is a further element in the book – and in its predecessor – that seeks to make a larger political case. And it is a point addressed as much to myself as to anyone else. Like others I began my career as a naturalist nearly fifty years ago with a desire to encounter as many exotic or charismatic creatures and plants as I possibly could across the world: satyr tragopans, tigers, birds-of-paradise, African rock pythons, marine iguanas, morpho butterflies, welwitschia (plants). Somehow I assumed that meaning and significance were entailed in the organism's rarity, or in its distance from my everyday world.

I have been privileged to see all the remarkable organisms named above. Perhaps as a consequence, but also because of the passage of time, I have come to realise that the extraordinariness in those species is also to be found here in oaks, common toads, blackbirds, brown hares, garden cross spiders, winter gnats. All are equally significant representatives of the processes of life that have a lineage stretching back for 3.8 billion years into an eon of the Earth's history known as the Archean.

I am increasingly conscious how, on hearing the songs of toads or blackbirds, I am placed in intimate connection with the life and times of the Jurassic age. In fact, it is now established that the latter is not just *related* to the dinosaurs, as I say in one of my March pieces, it *is* a dinosaur. In meeting any part of life we are privileged to understand, through the work of biologists and life scientists, that all of life is entailed in any encounter. Its whole heritage is, in a sense, omnipresent. In Papua New Guinea and in Claxton.

We pass our days bound into this great star-driven commerce. So far we have yet to split open a meteorite, or recover a rock from Mars, or the Moon, and find so much as a single example of unicellular life. The miracle is here, now, all about us. A passage from Henry Thoreau serves as a kind of credo for my response to this. If one first expands its nineteenth-century patriarchal bias to include us all, I think it carries enormous meaning. 'The man of most science,' he wrote, 'is the man most alive, whose life is the greatest event.' I take it to mean that the more we enquire, the more we notice what is about us, living and related to us, the more fully and truly we shall live. The book you hold in your hands is offered in this spirit.

# JANUARY

### ∞ CLAXTON, NORFOLK ∞

It came over our hedge and performed a slow swerve around me, a flying creature the size of a snowdrop's bloom, but rotund and black except for pale detail at the abdomen tip. I was so shocked I looked round for someone to receive the instantaneous and extraordinary tidings: a bumblebee at New Year!

What on Earth can such a sighting mean? I'll add detail to justify any unease in that question. It was probably one of two common species, buff-tailed or early bumblebee. Based on its small size I might have suggested the latter, but I keep records of spring firsts and my earliest-ever early bumblebee is late March. My earliest-ever bumblebee of any species is 28 January 2012: a whole month later than this one. In fact, I wondered if it were not so much premature as a veteran of last autumn. Whichever is true, it was a bumblebee in a seasonal no man's land and my strangest record of this insect family in half a century.

I wonder what causal chain I have to invoke to account for such a maladapted vision? Must the moment draw in its wake, if only by implication, all the ecological fallout from 5,000 million tonnes of carbon, which our species propels, car journey by car journey, flicked switch by flicked switch, into the troposphere every year? Or is it something else? Is my weird record connected to the weather anomalies generated by exceptional warm-water currents in the eastern Pacific? To think that there could be a link between that ocean's habits and my garden's wildlife is extraordinary enough, but at least a bumblebee because of El Niño is natural and, thus, admissible.

For much of recorded history, 'unnatural' events at the point of the year's renewal were often taken as ominous portents. I suspect little has changed. In our own ecologically informed age, when we understand how everything is linked to everything else, we may no longer resort to supernatural powers or the will of God to explain such freaks. Yet still we sense instinctively that a midwinter bumblebee can be neither random nor without meaning.

3 January 2017

⤌ THURSFORD, NORFOLK ⤍

A friend and fellow wood-owner has built a hide in his patch that's sunk into the ground so that the windows, which are fitted with one-way glass, look out at eye level over a nearby pond. From its interior you have the most intimate ringside views of the wildlife while the latter, meanwhile, has no inkling of human presence.

As we settled in and waited for the sun to rise and illuminate the spot, a dozen blackbirds breakfasted on the trolley-load of apples that were dumped around the pond. The birds hammered the fruits with gusto then they would pause, hammer again, sending white-flesh fids flying in all directions. Sometimes they sallied off completely, leaving a contrail of metallic sound ricocheting nervously among the trees. Silence descended; before all were suddenly back at once. They gulped more apple, head up, then down, and then a pause for a personal squabble with more scraped-metal chiding; or more nerves and off they sailed.

This fruit-feeding alternated with other jerky, leaf-flicking stuff, the slate pin legs scratching mud in tandem with a downward stab and sideways flick of the lemon-edged bill.

Occasionally one would break off from the staccato rhythms of the group and position itself so close to the glass that as you leant forward you felt sure she was looking at you as intently as you could see her.

Every detail was unmissable – the stained-oak eye, the sepia cup beneath her throat, her bird-track streaks running away down the chest into the fulsome shadows of her belly and then that sprung-loaded legs-out, chest-up posture that looked one part gun's cocked trigger, one part coiled-spring for flight. It was fabulous stuff.

As we sat and luxuriated in all this wild closeness you realised that we spend all our lives, not so much in shelter, but in a force field of fearsomeness that radiates from us into the world around. Our four-million-year-long heritage as top predatory ape has left us encircled by a dead penumbra of other creatures' dread. J. A. Baker wrote that, like all humans, he seemed to move 'within a hoop of red hot iron, a hundred yards across, that sears away all life'. It was grand to escape it just for a day.


6 January 2014

⊶ BUCKENHAM, NORFOLK ⊷

I was fascinated to observe the wigeon flock at this wetland site follow a distinct behavioural pattern as each day progressed. Mornings would find the ducks slewed along the course of the Yare and initially there were about 2,000. The low-angled sunlight reduced them to mere black blobs spread across the curl and slap of the sparkling river. Periodically a passing raptor – a marsh harrier or peregrine – would convulse them skywards and with each panic the total would decline a fraction. Birds peeled away in sun-dazzled mobs to settle on the various dykes that bisected the marsh.

The sub-groups would initially mill on the water and preen. With such vast unblemished skies and the light now perfectly angled, the dykes were converted to intense lines of Greek blue. The ducks too were saturated in winter sun and it enflamed the horse-chestnut red of the drake's head. It flared in the softer lion beige of his crown. Then there were the glorious red-deer browns of the duck's breast and face. In truth the pleasure of wigeon – perhaps of all duck plumage – is that their feathers never create simple planes of colour. Her face and chest are freckled in cream or black; what seems pale grey on a male's back and flanks is, in reality, a thousand sinuous charcoal lines over white.

As the afternoon wore through, the clean wild piping that gives wigeon their name and always surrounds them in an aura of innocence and comedy had dwindled to the odd throaty grumble. And these were just the complaints of singletons, birds in brief dispute with a neighbour. By mid-afternoon all were asleep and but for my increasingly cold nose and the steam intensifying with each exhalation, there was an air of summer contentment to these scenes. I suspect all this sunlit peacefulness was a product of wider astronomical conditions. Such was the cloudlessness of our nights that the wigeon could feed in the cold safekeeping of the moonlight and immune from the attentions of aerial predators.

6 January 2015

⋙ Claxton, Norfolk ⋘

I pulled the zip as high as it would go on my down jacket and took the white-frosted path to the River Yare. I was out to catch something of the soundscape in the last light, with the moon's reflection in Carleton Beck following me down for half a mile as a watery half-coin on its surface. The first sound of the marsh came from a snipe jinking and twisting low over the ground. Its undersides blinked momentarily white among the general brown vision of its going and, as it flew, it let out that series of small gruff snipe monosyllables – notes so rudimentary they're just dirt made into noise – until they were lost beneath the chorus from the wigeon on the river.

These duck were immersed in a cloud of their high sweet whistled calls. The individual note of each one has a slewed, trailing-away quality like a glass bottle skidding on thick ice. It also has an upwardly inflected interrogative tone, yet in concert the sounds created an answering reassurance for the whole flock and there was a wonderfully settled aura to their steady drift downstream. I could hear those softly murmured questions almost to the end of my walk and until there was just a final glow in the southern sky.

Out of this warm-toned horizon came the sound I'd come to see: the distant silence of a woodcock. So far the winter has been poor for this northern wader. Occasionally, when startled during daylight at their roosts in wet ground among sallows, woodcock rise vertically in alarm. These winter birds utter no call, except that as they come up the wings make a strange clean snick sound like a linen sheet pulled taut. If one could drill down into the actual cell structure of the bird it would be possible to locate geochemical signatures that would pinpoint its origins to some very specific Russian marsh or Swedish bog. Here tonight, however, it's just a fleeting boreal mystery – a heart and wings made from worms and, thus, of mud – silhouetted briefly in a Norfolk sky.

9 January 2012

CLAXTON, NORFOLK

I pass them every day on my way to the marsh and have completely failed to spot them. Yet they are so withered and are so much the tannin-brown colour of the stark limbs of these oaks that I can forgive myself the omission. There are two swinging gently at a twig end like some tiny forgotten gnarled fruits. In fact they are known as 'oak apples', small irregular spheres, similar to acorns in size, but they are no natural product of the tree.

Oak apples are galls created by an invasive insect, a type of cynipid wasp that lays eggs inside a leaf bud. The eggs cause the tree to respond vegetatively and a swollen tuber of hard material accumulates around the wasp larvae as they hatch. In time the canker-like outer shell provides protection for the developing grubs, while the inner tissue of the gall supplies their nutrients.

When I cut open the abandoned gall its interior unfolds as an interlocking mosaic of oval cells where dozens of larvae grew, developed and metamorphosed into adult wasps. These tunnelled out in midsummer and after mating they too deposited eggs that caused further gall growths on the oak's root system. It is within these secondary galls that another generation of asexual adults develops. About this time of year these wingless wasps emerge and climb the trunk in search of fresh leaf buds to begin the next generation of oak apple galls.

What I find most moving about these quiet fragments of our landscape is their venerable heritage. Margaret Redfern in her fabulous new book *Plant Galls* (HarperCollins) suggests that many gall wasps evolved in the Cretaceous, when flowering plants and herbivorous insects were diversifying. So when one notes an old oak apple swaying on a January breeze, one gets a glimpse not only into the miracle of life that was last summer, one peers into deep time, back to an age when the Earth was peopled with reptiles the size of oak trees.

16 January 2018

⤜ CLAXTON, NORFOLK ⤐

On any walk to the marsh I'm always struck how, with a single click of the closing door, the entire audible routine of our house interior – the ticking clock, the even hum of the central heating or fridge, the slow breathing of all that other civilised stuff – is washed away instantly by the sound tide of the outdoors.

What we perhaps require as an animal is release from that atmospheric certainty. Being outdoors permits an immersion in the unending and endlessly unpredictable music of nature, which the musician and naturalist Bernie Krause, in his book *The Great Animal Orchestra*, calls the 'biophony'. Perhaps it is this that restores the default settings of our species. We have been attuned to the Earth's wild song for 100,000 generations; why should we cease to want or need it after just ten spent mainly indoors?

One can hear the tempo and variety of winter sounds pick up even in the first flat days of the new year. Robins have never stopped all their customary sweetness but around us the great tits have renewed their enamelled two-note repertoire and song thrush song is just now being banged out by our local birds. However, the best seasonal sound of the parish still comes from the wintering pink-footed geese.

There were 400 in the last field before the River Yare. As I moved down the track they all suddenly burst up on their wings' broad acre. It was as if the field had uprooted and their calls were the landscape itself in full clamour. In a sense pinkfeet evoke two rather contradictory responses, because the full effect is made up by the repetition of a shrill doggish double-syllabled yap from each bird. We might hear it as a chorus but every sharp note is an appeal by a parent or an immature goose to its nearest relatives. All that northern noise is thus filled with familial feeling and excitement.

At the same time, big flocks of pinkfeet will vocalise for as long as they are airborne, and their outpourings seem to draw in something of the open heaven and the wind's own song. So the full performance is spacious and air-filled and as this flock spread and wound across the sky it enfolded all the blue above Claxton into the long intricate chain of wild-goose music.

## 17 January 2017

### ↬ Rockland St Mary, Norfolk ↫

Our neighbours have five acres of commercial apples that supply both the surrounding community in autumn and our thrush neighbours during winter.

Recently I fulfilled a long-held promise to erect a hide and watch them among the windfalls. Firstly I had to gather several barrowfuls of my own, which was itself a memorable exercise. While I raked the wasp-mined Bramleys my boots mulched down the flesh, sending up a sweet foetor and leaving geometrically patterned cakes of apple mud underfoot. Once I'd assembled 100 lbs of sweetness it was tipped in a sunlit heap by the hide, then I retired to steep the whole scene in silence, before returning next day.

The blackbirds found it first, although I could hear fieldfares all about. Befitting their relative physical proportions, the latter birds' calls are coarser and larger than blackbird notes. They also have a jarring quality, an element of awkwardness, resembling the sound of twisted rubber, as if some force of effort went into their making.

They are wilder than blackbird sounds without any hint of domestication, for fieldfares are a rough tribe from Europe's boreal woodlands. It's not uncommon to see two fight over fruit for minutes on end, each lunging alternately at the other as if strings controlled the patterned rise and fall of their squabble.

The flock slowly summoned the courage to feed as one, although sudden, hard-fletched panic was a common interruption. I came to appreciate how the *chakking* notes are a permanent anxiety-filled force field about fieldfares that governs their social lives and oversees their security. They maintain it with good reason: one morning I came back to find a sparrowhawk kill, a nest of beautiful feathers around the death spot.

But desire would eventually trump fear and down they plumped, mixing thick impasto ochres and burnt chocolate and smoky blue-greys into the lime greens and oranges of the rotting fruit. Yet this was not art but life and when all the birds were settled to feed, gulping simultaneously, heads and throats quivering as they snaked down apple pulp, the whole scene seemed to pullulate like a hill of maggots. It was an object lesson in survival, in the exigencies of thrush hunger and the imperishable abundance of an English winter.

19 January 2014

WAYLAND WOOD, NORFOLK

It might sound perverse but one thing I love about Wayland Wood just south of Watton on the A1075 is its maze-like riddle of footpaths. Part of this stems from the fact that the place is supposed to be the setting for the real events behind the story *Babes in the Wood*.

This old tale tells of an evil couple who contrive the death of their two wealthy stepchildren in order to steal the inheritance. Although the youngsters are spared a grisly murder at the hands of paid assassins, they wander forlornly along the woodland paths until their sad demise. The only consoling part is that the wild birds, out of pity, bury their tiny corpses under the leaves. A place that inspired such a dark tale should be large and entangled and perhaps a little spooky.

Alas Wayland is now too small for its old role. At its widest the five-sided patch of ash, oak and hazel coppice, which is owned by the Norfolk Wildlife Trust, is only 34 hectares in extent and 500 metres across. On one side you can hear the traffic roar from the A1075; on the other it's just the empty silence of sugarbeet fields.

While Wayland is certainly compact, the network of trails is still so wonderfully labyrinthine that I seldom make a circuit of the wood in exactly the same way twice. And getting lost at Wayland is the best way to discover its real magic. It is one of the region's oldest and most precious patches of ancient woodland.

The place is mentioned in the Domesday Book and was probably already many hundreds if not thousands of years old by the reign of William the Conqueror.

We have no problem investing reverence, meaning and importance in something as old as Norwich Cathedral. We have more trouble understanding a site like Wayland and approaching it with a due sense of appreciation. Yet, in truth, we should see both as equally precious.

Perhaps the reason we often don't is that we are so much more in love with our own creations than we are with those of nature; although Wayland is at least a product of partnership between ourselves and the trees. The place has been managed and harvested by human hand for more than a millennium. The main practice is called coppicing, when the trees are cut at their bases and then allowed to regrow in a spray of straight poles.

Often cut on an eight-to-fifteen-year rotation, these coppice poles grow quickly. In fact one reason why Wayland is so delightfully confounding is that it seems to change between each visit. Blocks of ground that were open last year are now filled with a dense screen of new growth. Contrary to its status as 'ancient woodland' there are precious few large trees to convey a sense of history. Signs of antiquity are more subtle and include the living tree stumps which spread and bulge just above the soil surface where the coppicing has recurred sometimes for centuries. In fact trees that are cut in this fashion can live longer than their 'wild' unadulterated peers.

Another aspect to ancient woods that is sometimes difficult to appreciate during a superficial visit is their variety. Yet ecosystems that enjoy the same recurrent management over extended periods acquire both stability and diversity. If ever we had a habitat that approximated to the much-celebrated rainforests of the tropics then ancient woodland is among our richest.

Swanton Novers just north of Wayland is another of the region's most important woods but it has been more extensively studied. So far it has been proven to hold more than 670 different species of beetle, 570 moths, 750 fungi and 350 plants. These are only indicators of its overall richness. My guess is that a site like Swanton Novers or Wayland could easily hold 6,000-plus different species, a tenth of the entire range of organisms in Britain.

The truth is we just don't know quite how diverse they are. To give a tiny example of the problem, during a recent visit to Wayland I turned up a wonderful but highly conspicuous bracket fungus for which there was no previous record. The real issue is not whether the animals occur but whether there are the specialist naturalists with time and opportunity to census properly a place like Swanton Novers or Wayland.

What we do know for certain is that such places cannot be reproduced. They are irreplaceable bastions of our living heritage. That's why it is profoundly troubling that the Environment Secretary Owen Paterson recently announced that in certain cases developers could offset the destruction of ancient woodland by planting twice as many trees. It suggests a deep indifference or ignorance on his part.

It is the equivalent of suggesting that one could knock down Norwich Cathedral as long as one erected a brand-new shiny structure elsewhere that was twice the size of the old one. In ecology as in religious architecture, novelty and size count for far less than the slow accretion of tradition and the patient creative passage of the years.

20 January 2013

⟜ HARDLEY FLOOD, NORFOLK ⟞

I love the way that the dusk comes to the Yare Valley and the way its ritualised patterns are even more emphasised in winter than they are in summer. One dominant rite is the solemn flow of gulls overhead. They come in their thousands, arrow-like lines or just shapeless mobs of birds converging from who knows which parts of Norfolk, to pass the cold hours at a roost near Yarmouth. The other strong counter current – since it heads north–south and not east–west like the gulls – is the evening stream of rooks and jackdaws to their own accustomed spot on the far bank at Buckenham. The Loddon flock drifts off, accompanied by a joyous rabble of contact notes, at exactly 4.07 p.m.

Here at Hardley there is now a gathering air of tension. I watch the flocks of mallard, gadwall, wigeon, pintail and shelduck until they are reduced to mere duck-shaped cavities of darkness upon the water. Yet the greylag geese greet nightfall with a kind of growing frenzy. Their coarse braying calls build to a climax and it comes as a relief when they finally clatter the lake surface and heave northwards in a fresh access of panic. The going allows my attention to settle on the landscape's last formalities. On every side the woods echo to blackbirds and pheasants that release their own anxieties in an hysterical commonwealth of alarm notes. Only at last light do they finally recover composure and lapse into silence.

I wander back along the mud-clagged trail where a tissue of ice already closes over all. Then an owl emerges and I pause. It swoops down over the reeds in a shallow curve on wings that seem as broad as they are long, and rises to the bushes beyond. There follows shortly another owl's arc but this one is made of sound. The unmistakable wavering, soft, drawn-out bow of its song, which robes the entire landscape in a last layer of darkness; and night falls.

## 20 January 2015

### ⤙ CLAXTON, NORFOLK ⤚

There is little in this morning's landscape that looks more lifeless than the withered heads of the old nettles. Yet one should not forget how even they, as they chaff and creak in the breeze, and when joined by the reed or sedge all around, create that typical soft woodwind accompaniment to winter. In his essay 'Nature',

Emerson wrote: 'The stars of the dead calices of flowers, and every withered stem and stubble rimed with frost, contribute something to the mute music.'

In that same spirit I try now not to overlook the visual pleasures of winter plants. On the track to the marsh the lesser burdock stems are hugely suggestive. The hook-tipped heads have an armoury that conjures something darkly medieval, or perhaps just spikes of light radiating from a source. In truth even these dry husks are full of life purpose. Brush them with a woolly cuff or even the pleated wrist of a cagoule and the seeds are instant migrants in search of new land.

A favourite winter bloom is common hogweed. It lacks the flourish of last year's teasel or the height of dead hemlock, but there is something captivating about its surviving architecture. The main stem is entirely hollow and the side umbels all desiccated but the overlapping star-shaped patterns have the same intricacies of the living plant. Yet the atmosphere is of a valiant last stand, rather than of any future promise.

Real hope is left to the only gorse bush on this track. In truth it creates a sense of assurance mingled with mystery. Why on Earth does it bloom now? Come April it will be festooned with furrow-spider webs. Its immediate atmosphere will carry a dancing cloud of St Mark's flies and the entire bush will be wreathed in linnet song or bombarded by the crazy tropical music of sedge warblers. But now its little world is shriven of all other life and even that delicious scent of coconuts is purged by cold wind. All I can say is that those glorious papilionaceous flowers, burning yellow against that January blue, are warmer than the sun itself.

25 January 2016

⤕ ROCKLAND ST MARY, NORFOLK ⤔

Traditionally each village in the Broads had what is called a 'staithe', a tiny port linking it commercially to the wider regional river system. Rockland's is among the prettiest: a rectangular tidal pool, edged with steel-plate revetments and dotted with mooring posts, to which are attached idle dayboats with names like *Windsong*.

On one side is a young oak grove that remains an almost permanent sump of winter shadow gathered over a lawn all neatly mown and with two slatted benches. Aside from the odd fisherman plodding to his pitch, the grove is entirely untenanted and quiet, but for its one winter robin and, now, a female kestrel.

It is an odd haunt for her, but one can hardly overstate this falcon's versatility. The stock hover-and-pounce vole-hunting method of kestrels can overwhelm anything from crows to bats or dragonflies. I once saw one steal prey from a short-eared owl in a high aerial dogfight, while their daylight robbery of barn owls is so commonplace it often forces the owls to hunt by night. Yet this female was seeing out the grinding cloud-brewed misery of the month by catching worms.

The technique involves sitting under the trees, over the turf, the dozen rusty bars of her black-striped mantle-feathers puffed out for comfort, where she waits. Waits and watches, eyes always angled relentlessly down. Then she drops, silver underwings flashing even in the submerged watery gloom, and then pounces, twisting foot to beak, and pulling on the lank pink flesh. Then a bill wipe and up in more deft silver strokes, and we are soon all as we were, minute by sodden minute.

It was odd to reflect that there was an underlying relationship between those light-filled movements and that worm-fuel energy. All that elan was, in effect, earth-eaters and, thus, soil itself. I suppose that a secondary element in this ecological moment is the words on kestrel movement that now muscle and sinew out of this article into your brain. In a way your imaginings of a kestrel's dogged survival in these sullen times, like the bird itself, are all just emanations processed from the same wet soil.

## 30 January 2018

### WINTERTON, NORFOLK

Walking along the beach at this wonderful National Nature Reserve, we were struck by the extraordinary sense of volatile energy in the sea, sky and land. Everything and everyone – the gulls cycling relentlessly over the waves, the seals ashore and the strollers along the beach – were all bathed in brilliant sun dazzle.

Yet the air was filled with salt spray and whipped-up sand and the dune vegetation all shuddered in a high wind. At the water's edge, out of every freshly smashed wave, the northerlies scooped out mounds of foam that were then washed ashore with the tide when it looked as if a trowel had smoothed them down as a fresh layer of white across the flats.

Regardless of the perpetual churn there was also extraordinary stillness and the dark eyes of the grey-seal pups seemed its very soul. Many were born last month and while some still have the creamy lanugo of birth, others have already moulted and acquired pebbly grey spots on their bellies and backs.

Their increase in size is remarkable, individuals gaining as much as 1.8 kg a day from the 50 per cent fat of their mother's milk. I love the way these youngsters loll on their backs with not a care in this frenzied world and when I zoomed a lens into the face of one sleeping pup you could see how the left nostril flared open with each rhythmic exhalation, like an old man snoring contentedly.

Not all the seals were at ease. Adult females may have only just given birth but the reproductive strategy of the species is remorseless and they are usually pregnant again even before they wean the winter's pups. To make sure of it the bulls patrol the beach for any receptive partner.

Seal sex is a highly public and rather fraught business. Even in congress the heads and upper bodies of both animals writhe and, open mouthed, they snarl and gnash at each other's face. His scarred neck is covered in gore, her bared teeth curve into a strange sort of smiling grimace. Then they slumber down, his flipper on her flank, and she nuzzles in so that their long whiskers momentarily intertwine.

# FEBRUARY

2 February 2016

CLAXTON, NORFOLK

What is it about owls that is so captivating? I'm sure one part of the allure is that array of night noises which passes for owl communication. Frequently we have barn owls land on our bedroom roof, where they delight in waking us with a coarse breathy hiss that sounds like something concocted by a zombie coming out of the crypt in an old Hammer horror film. *Earhhhhhh!*

Even better is tawny owl song, which has begun this week and is the earliest marker of winter's breakdown. It reminds me in one specific sense of its diurnal twin, the cockerel's dawn clarion. They both arc across the sky and fall towards you out of some indeterminate space. Owl sounds are a language purified of all visual nuance and gesture. They are intense on the ear and impenetrable to our understanding and like a flash of lightning in the night storm they manage paradoxically to make the darkness clearer but more unfathomable.

The other thing about owls is their binocular vision. In most birds the eyes are so widely spaced on the head you see only a single iris at any one time. With owls they seem to watch us as much as we look at them. It is the piercing glare of equals: a mutual pondering on otherness and similarity. Even when their eyes are shut in that bizarre love-heart-shaped facial disc, they seem able to compel us.

Recently I was in Kikinda in northern Serbia, where up to 750 long-eared owls – part of this species' largest concentration on the planet – roost every night in the town's main streets. By the bank ATM next to our hotel there were twenty-three in one tree, but along the fence of the infant school I counted thirty. At dawn the entire town is caught in sunlit hoar frost and as the residents stroll to work or their lessons, they thread through the parallel world of these night birds. The owls are utterly indifferent, their eyelids squeezed tight like closed shutters, holding aloof from the human community and stopping up in the darkness of their dreams all that gloriously unknowable magic of their lives.

## 3 February 2014

### ❦ Savernake Forest, Wiltshire ❦

Although this former royal forest is most famous for its beeches, which rise like gigantic organ pipes 30 metres overhead, we were on the search for bigger quarry. Among this landscape of clay-rooted tree and squirrel and muntjac and white-barred brambling sifting beech mast on the woodland floor, there are a dozen or so ancient, quietly cloistered oaks at Savernake. It took us ages to find the Cathedral Oak, a glorious twelve-trunked brute that was jammed tight against a chain-link fence, which seemed far too everyday a context for so venerable an organism. The tree is reputed to date to the Norman Conquest.

Not so the mossy, club-footed veteran known as Old Paunchy, which, at several hundred years, is a mere stripling in comparison with the others. As we stood before the Big Belly Oak, a hollowed-out monster with a great steel brace around its midriff, we pondered what it was they made us feel and why.

The temptation is to name them all as beautiful, but Big Belly Oak has the coarse fissured surfaces of a huge dinosaur. If a stegosaurus were ever beautiful then so is this tree. Another strong urge is to say that they are magnificent but, in truth, they are often also squat, solid, asymmetrical and without regularity of feature, grace or bright colour.

Is it perhaps more the fact that each took a billion acorns to produce, or that they contain all of our post-Norman human history in one wood stump? Or is it our time-lapse reflections on all those billions of other organisms that have lived and flourished in their complex embrace over the last millennium? Could it also be that they turn death into a sort of living process? The extraordinary oak called King of Limbs has been shedding branches, rotting slowly down for decades, and possibly centuries. It is finally – and surely? – that they simply *are*. They endure. And in their presence we can only stand and wonder at all that they have been and into what future they will journey still long after we have ceased to be.


## 3 February 2015

### ⋘ WAXHAM, NORFOLK ⋙

Although the thirty grey seals that have hauled out to breed at this spot may collectively weigh 10 tonnes, they look little more than a low-lying hoard on the dipping horizon of beach and tide. Even on close approach they are just a third of the height of the final waves cresting ashore and in these February temperatures and with a bitter north wind spitting sand, they look like gigantic fish-bloated larvae marinated in contentment.

I love the way one sings that soft low moan like wind through sand. I love even more how another will heave up its head momentarily, the mottled brown-and-cream pelt breadcrumbed in sand, and graze a flipper over an ample flank. Or even its neighbour's. Then it flicks its chin with that five-nailed comb like an Edwardian gent adjusting his whiskers and slumps down softly. Who could imagine that this suggestive wallow of life could be such box office, yet the wardens tell me that over the winter more than 43,000 people have come to see the seals.

Occasionally they threaten genuine drama. One big bull, fresh out of the spume and shovelling the moleskin black of his bulk up the beach, has mouth open and his huge dog's teeth, which can kill porpoise or grind down seven kilos of cod a day, unsheathed. Then he yawns, rolls over, his pink grin turns upside down, and from my angle the beast becomes a huge jellied ball compressed by gravity. Perhaps there is a kind of imaginative theatre underneath all that fat: when he finally lumbers back to the water, whose cold could kill us within the hour, he could swim, if he wished, all the way to Northumberland or sail offshore to Europe.

Yet I suspect the human crowds are coming less to marvel than to dote. Nestled higher up the beach are the pups, whose immense liquid eyes seem even darker against the whiteness of their lanugo. While they await the 50 per cent fat of their mothers' milk they doze in an atmosphere of winter dazzle and icy sun and the sugared *oohs* and *aahs* of brief human affections.

## 7 February 2017

### ⤚ CLAXTON, NORFOLK ⤛

It is not dense enough to call mist let alone fog, but February's invisible damp gives milkiness to the air and weight to the morning's mood, so that the ivy leaves in our hedge seem to droop as if they have all been licked downwards and our garden robin hugs their shadow with its brown back to me. As I walk to the river I notice that the oak leaves by the track, which were frosted copper last month, are in mid journey from leaf mulch to soil.

Across the marsh there is no division between the grey of the sky and land, and, thus, no horizon and even the dark of the woods is burred with softness. The north-westerly is mild and lifts only the lightest vegetation – the reed tops by the sides of the path – and the moisture adds to each intake of breath the cold savour of bare earth and dead leaves.

There are birds – jackdaws yakking and rooks somewhere with their stone-shovelling music – but they are the bog standards at this season. The one unfamiliar detail is a JCB on the far side that has been slubbing out the dykes. Now its operations have temporarily ceased and from here, with the bucket buried in reed and its long neck outstretched, it looks like some weird yellow giant's corpse locked in rigor mortis.

These dead-quiet spells of late winter involve days of no change but I love to reflect that most of spring is here but hidden somewhere in all this quiescence. In a fortnight, frogs will crawl from under stones to breed. In a month, the toads will float up from the bottom of the dykes to sing. The grass snakes that curl at the water's edge and sunbathe by late March are sleeping underground and the hoverflies that hum about the sallow blossoms by the track are buried in mud. The bare trees, even the barbed wire of the hawthorns, will soon bud and, while the swallows that nest near the manor are probably in Namibia or South Africa now, they are already moulted and have acquired that miraculous blue, which they will bring to us soon across 6,000 miles.

## 16 February 2016

### ⤜ BLACKWATER CARR, NORFOLK ⤛

The other day I was using my crome in one of the dykes. It is a tool dating to the Middle Ages with a name said to derive from Celtic (*crom* meant 'crooked'). Although it was a gift from a friend it sometimes feels like a curse. The thick ash handle is well over 2 metres long and the heavy iron head resembles a massive fork, but the tines bend at more than 90 degrees back from the line of the shaft.

It is used for dragging out slub and vegetation but the worst opponent is common reed. Flag irises or sedges have shallow roots that sit at the water's surface and with a fair heave they can be landed cleanly. But reeds prefer to fight for their lives. They sink white tuberous roots, like elephantine bamboo shoots, deep into the dyke bottom. Reeds require that you battle both the dense surface flotilla and then all those submerged root reinforcements. You heave, they 'pull' in the opposite direction until you are leaning back at 60 degrees. Any moment you could fall over backwards. More often it feels as if the reed is pulling you in. Then it gives and up the bank surges a great mud-fish, sometimes 10 kg in weight, sodden, with wriggling root barbels at its oozing mud mouth.

This time it gifted me something special. A water shrew was sneezed violently out of the battle zone of crome and reed. All silky dark fur and squirming energy on the water's duckweed surface, it looked like a paintbrush head writhing through green impasto paint. Shrews are all sex and death and astonishing life. The male's balls can be a tenth of his body weight. A lactating female can eat twice her own weight in a day. The bite is venomous. The flesh is acrid, thus, when the teeth finally wear through and the shrew starves to death, the corpse often lies completely untouched. I regularly see common shrews on autumn roads. But this water shrew was Blackwater's first. It scrawled itself momentarily all over that micro-landscape, then I was alone again with the joy of its fierce pygmy's exit.

## 17 February 2014

### ⤙ CLAXTON, NORFOLK ⤚

The corvid roost at Buckenham Carrs is an extraordinary phenomenon. Every night from October until February the jackdaws and rooks from an area of about 400 square kilometres of the Norfolk Broads drain steadily out of their many individual sites dotted across the parishes, into a series of ever-increasing pre-roost flocks. Come the hour before dusk, the entire regional population is probably in a dozen fields. By the end of evening all those birds are together in one wood, while the surrounding countryside is devoid of either species.

I find it moving to reflect that, as I watch 'my' birds concentrate near our house, exactly the same process is unfolding nationwide. If you look out of your window at dusk today wherever you may be in these islands, from Wick and Stornoway to Lydd and Landewednack, you will catch some fragment of this same flocking process.

The only difference is that the Buckenham roost probably involves more birds. Exactly how many is a matter of debate but it is probably never less than 40,000 and seldom as high as the largest claims (80,000). What is indisputable is the beauty and power of the spectacle, which is all the more moving for comprising merely a load of old crows. The basic vision that so many birds present to the spectator is a graceful flowing of wings enfolded within the wider ocean of their contact calls. When this torrid movement circles high in the blue it seems a gloriously slow black ballet of repeated shapes. When it dips lower over the wood, as it does tonight, it achieves a nice tension with the up-thrusting architecture of the bare trees. These create a crazed pattern of fracture lines whose stillness measures and gives context to the modulated current of birds. Steadily as this last flight unfolds, one pattern amalgamates with the other until you are left with a final resolution: a sweep of winter trees foliated with birds and softened by the velvet darkness of their voices.

### 18 February 2013

#### CLAXTON, NORFOLK

Technically we know that within four weeks the brimstones will emerge and in three the first queen bumblebees will sway low across the turf as they hunt for nest sites. But for now all is gridlocked in this icy south wind. Although the dykes are unfrozen their edges are gelid and the February air is smoky and hard-glazed and somehow deader now than November's. The southerly rolls through the Yare Valley and where it rises up the riverbank it works at the old dry stems of marsh sow thistle and teasel, so that these stumps nod relentlessly back and forth in that repeated rocking action one associates with the depressed.

The cold blast smears all sounds of birds and they are blurred into the sough of wind, all, that is, except for the common gulls. At this time of year they start to enact the rituals that will accompany breeding and it includes paired birds nodding and swaying in unison or raising their heads in synchrony to release a high modulated wailing note that is full of emotional ambiguity and occupies that place where hysterical laughter meets despair.

The birds' appearance has also acquired touches of the nesting season. Their heads and necks are pure white (but were grey smudged last autumn) and the dove-grey mantles and wings somehow cleaner and brighter. We often overlook the aesthetics of gulls and assume that the chromatic range in their plumage is too narrow for true beauty. It is usually some version of grey mingled with white. Yet we should not forget how the birds redeem those tones from their human associations. To see a flock of common gulls afloat on updraughts above sea cliffs, the birds rising in loose shoals high into the blue, is to appreciate grey unlocked from any residual sense of concrete, bureaucracy, conformity or boredom. Gulls make grey beautiful again and for now it is all I have to tell me that things will improve and that spring comes.

20 February 2018

❦ SHAPWICK, SOMERSET ❦

In any other place a great white egret passing overhead would have commanded all our attention. The national breeding total for this species was just seven pairs in 2017. Here, however, at dusk it was an incidental detail, a stately white shape rowing quietly through the binoculars' orbit, as we focused on something far more captivating.

It was a flock of starlings, which doesn't sound impressive until you attach a number to them. The recent reports cite a figure of 750,000. Yet in conversation with a volunteer from a neighbouring reserve we learnt that this estimate doesn't square with his own photographic evidence. He processes the images using special software that can calculate dots on screens very accurately and his own counts suggest a total for the whole Somerset Levels of around 1.5 million.

Whichever figure is true, this roost of 'shitlegs' is a wonder to behold, and for us the drama unfolded in several distinct phases. Initially we were entranced simply to see several thousands, spread evenly through the sky and moving in a slow blizzard above the skeletal trees. The stillness of the winter wood, the chastening cold of dusk and the clanging notes of song thrushes at late choir were all part of the moment's affecting mood. Then a sparrowhawk shot through and the loose flow tightened and folded upon itself, twisting and spiralling down, genie-like, into the mothering woods.

Wonderful, we thought – until thousands became tens, and then hundreds, of thousands of birds, and we were struggling for words. They were birds reduced by distance and number to something like smoke in a long slow globular unfolding that seemed as solid and fulsome as the vegetation or the ground over which it flowed. There were such astonishing numbers as dreams are made of. Starlings turning like a tide; except that this tide flipped suddenly into itself to make a glorious nonsense of any metaphor. It was a kind of heaven in avian form. As we stood and watched we felt uplifted merely to be there, immersed in a susurration that is blended from two million small wings working as one at end of day.

21 February 2013

<>◌ CLAXTON, NORFOLK ◌<>

Imagine, if you will, this typical autumn scene. You are off to the woods to hunt for a basket of sweet chestnuts. Across the intervening fields where green spikes of barley already break the earth, you flush pheasants and red-legged partridges as you walk. A trio of hares jinks away, their awkward limbs and fantastical ears all dancing on the far horizon. Rabbits bolt for cover every ten paces and at one particularly fine old sweet chestnut you're caught in the searchlight beam of a little owl's piercing yellow glare.

When the bird bounds away it draws your eye to the white scuts of a dozen fallow deer trotting for the anonymity of the deeper wood. A few metres more and there is your sweet chestnut harvest scattered over the earth like tiny green sputniks that have just showered down from outer space.

Could you think of a scene more intrinsically rural, more quintessentially English than this? And if you cannot, then think again. All the constituents of that imaginary landscape are there because of us. They are what environmentalists call non-native species. Barley came with our Neolithic forebears; the hares and chestnuts were imports of the Iron Age; the Normans gave us the deer, rabbits and pheasants; the partridges first arrived with Charles II, while the owl had to wait for a few sympathetic Victorians to make its English entrée. Yet all are now deeply embedded in our sense of the countryside.

The affections that such plants and animals awaken comment obliquely upon the present orthodox environmental position, which disallows the introduction of all non-native species. The release of aliens is even illegal, their presence is invariably condemned and now the price of their invasion has been economically quantified ('"Alien" wildlife in Europe wreaks €12bn damage a year', *Guardian* 21 February 2013).

There are undoubtedly strong reasons for the current position on aliens. Our introduction of non-native plants and animals has had some devastating consequences. The classic locus for this mayhem is isolated islands, of which Hawaii is the perfect example. Biologically unique, this Pacific archipelago once held perhaps 145 bird species found nowhere else on Earth.

Today only thirty-five still exist and twenty-four of those are endangered. Of a grand total of 22,000 animals and plants found in the Hawaiian islands, 4,373 are aliens. Yet the true villains among this invading horde to Hawaii's paradisiacal ecosystem are relatively few. They include domestic pigs, rats, mosquitoes, the avian malaria protozoa and the appropriately named big-headed ant.

The problem with such undeniable evidence of aliens' baleful impact is that it can lead to a knee-jerk response to all non-native species. It reinforces a binary moral vision of nature – indigenous/good and alien/bad – that over-simplifies an often complex picture.

My earlier chestnut-hunting scenario makes that case nicely. Who would ever argue now that sweet chestnut trees are undesirable aliens? A wood such as Felbrigg in north Norfolk, owned by the National Trust, where 300-year-old veterans reach out to the heavens with vast gnarled arthritic limbs, is one of the most beautiful woodland environments in the country. Rabbits may have played hell with the Australian outback but they are fundamental to the maintenance and ecology of Britain's last grassland environments, cropping the sward with their relentless incisors, creating perfect conditions for ground-nesting birds and maintaining floral diversity.

As for the hare, who could imagine spring even arriving at all without that creature's madcap capering antics? Yet there is a mammal that argues even more strongly for a nuanced approach to non-native invaders. The Chinese water deer is a primitive Labrador-sized species with strange vampire's canines that escaped into the East Anglian landscape in the mid twentieth century.

Exotic though it may sound, this endearing creature with teddy bear's ears is now integral to the Broads environment. Where I live the winter nights are filled with the wild music of its courtship calls. Today, this alien mammal population may be fundamental to the species' existence, given the parlous condition of the deer in its native Asian range. Britain's Chinese water deer may yet become its last best hope for survival.

So we should continue to bless the hare as a bringer of spring and learn to love the Chinese water deer as a new, permanent resident in our midst. Ultimately, though, we should avoid a blanket condemnation of 'aliens' and take each case – each non-native species – on its individual merits.

## 21 February 2017

### ⤜ BLACKWATER CARR, NORFOLK ⤚

Although I am in my fifties I still take a child's pleasure in climbing trees. This particular ascent, however, had purpose because a hawthorn formerly trapped under a sallow thicket has been steadily freed by felling operations. Yet one last branch had to be severed before my overtopped bush could move into the sunlit uplands of the open glade that I have created around it.

There are four hawthorns and one small holly honoured in this fashion. They receive preferential treatment partly because they are rare on my patch, but also because I cherish the idea that they are bird sown. I like to imagine the scenario that explains their presence in a sallow jungle: the fruit-filled blackbird, perhaps, that returned night after night to roost and deposited the undigested hawthorn and holly seeds that it had eaten during the day. Out of its shower of creative manure there eventually arose my new bushes.

Once you are attuned to this avian tree propagation it becomes part of the detective's pleasure in unravelling nature to find other instances of the same process. There are excellent examples in our garden because the blackthorn hedge I planted fifteen years ago now has an understorey of elder and holly breaking out along its length. They are almost certainly the work of our garden thrushes and, rather than grub them out, I leave them to their own devices so that our garden is a creative process shared by its various owners.

Our whole village is liberally speckled not only with hollies but many of the houses and even some local farms are named after the same species. So, in a sense the birds have helped to shape the cultural texture of the parish as well as the physical landscape. In this island kingdom we are so accustomed to the notion that we own and can stamp our authority on all its parts yet, beyond our superficial gaze, there is still another landscape fashioned by birds and trees. It is in this sense that I also think of my tree climbing as a political act in the service of a wilder republic.

# MARCH

I March 2016

As my poor mother's eyes mist over with cataracts I give constant thanks for my own sight. This morning as I heard wild swans bugling faintly high over the house I thought also of friends who now have to have hearing devices in their ears. Yet what of our sense of smell? Isn't it, of all the senses, the most underrated?

The perfume that leads me to ponder all this has the power of music to awaken so much personal history. For some reason it is a smell that returns me instantly to a time in my twenties and winter mornings in Nepal, but it also contains a hint of any place that I have seen where the houses are timber-made and where traffic noise is absent. It is also the very essence of autumn and as central to that season as those childhood hoards of dead leaves so high-piled in the woods that we could almost swim through them.

It is not just my past I can identify, but all of our pasts. I remember thinking in Benin in West Africa once how this very odour implied change to whole continents. Its consequences were laid out like an immense blackened beast over the entire countryside. At its edges it was all yellow toothed and devouring the vegetation, while overhead through the crackling heat-haze, and the wisps of black ash carried on their billowing hot-air cushion, came bee-eaters and kites to snatch insects fleeing before its advance.

The smell of which I speak is, in a sense, the scent of all human culture. Not just the cave's thick atmosphere that blurred the Paleolithic images flickering on the walls. It is the smell of cooked food, the smithy's forge and the combustion of steam. It is still there implied in all those things brewed by industry and now it is a smell about our entire future. It is the aroma that turned carbon into the dark cloud hanging over us all. It has just the faintest whiff of calving icebergs and even a vision of polar bears, all white wool and sagging bones in pools of melted ice. Yet, strangely, it is one of my favourite fragrances: woodsmoke, from logs that I cut from our trees and stack and burn, to keep us warm all winter long.

## 3 March 2015

### ⌁ NORTON MARSHES, NORFOLK ⌁

Something was afoot among the hares in these fields. Three of a quartet were sunk to ground, ears flattened to their backs. Aside from the frog's bulge of their half-closed eyes – whose long slits reminded me of those unearthly faces in West African fetish masks – their owners could have been old weathered molehills.

Yet a singleton was upright and alert, his barrel chest bright ginger in the direct sun and those ludicrous ears sending stripes of darker shade across the brindled back. As they rotated I could see how the ears' curves caught the shadows at their shell centre and I wondered which of the world's nuances were being funnelled into the mysterious chambers of a hare's brain.

He was restless. In fact even the other three intermittently came back to life to groom and scratch, before collapsing once more. Hare kinetics has a strangely involuntary quality. It is as if all that compressed energy and those coiled limbs cannot be contained at will. They need some occasional outlet. There was one glorious moment when the singleton made full stretch, the ears spiked back and the hind legs pulled to their fullest extent, with the beautiful white bow of the belly drawn taut behind the ribs. Briefly this mammal had the weird proportions of a grasshopper and one sensed that such a luxurious arc of limb should be a yogic posture – the Hare, perhaps: good for breath control and stretching sinew.

Weirder still was a cycling action he performed with his forelimbs. They rotated in sequence with the speed and rhythm of a boxer rattling a punchbag. Then he trotted off, levered up at intervals by the crazy disproportion of his back legs. How strange that an animal built for speed seems to limp when it walks. He came back and sank down. An hour later no one, including me, had really moved. As I drove home and the new moon cut its white curve in the blue-black of nightfall, I imagined them there in the dark: poised and sculptural with outstretched limbs like a sphinx, yet restless still.

## 5 March 2013

### CLAXTON, NORFOLK

My trips to the bottle bank usually make for interesting natural historical excursions. In summer the empties and jars have an assorted burden of slugs and snails, which I try to salvage before they vanish into the bank's thickly whiskered maw. In winter the mice somehow get into our storage bins to enjoy the dregs and the residue of sugars. I am alerted to their visits by the droppings but also because they like to shred the plastic bags before slaking their thirst. Yet I have a suspicion that these nocturnal activities among our bottles are more than a calorific necessity in hard times. There is widespread evidence that animals other than ourselves enjoy alcohol.

The story of African elephants becoming inebriated on fermented marula fruits has more recently been debunked despite widespread historical claims. However a number of birds have been recorded to take pleasure in drink. There's a wonderful story of waxwings in North America so tanked up on rotting chokecherries that they tottered unsteadily along the branches using outstretched wings to balance, while some fell completely off their perches and could only respond to the observers by hissing like snakes. The bananaquit of Latin America also has a taste for alcohol of 4–6 per cent proof and an even more remarkable capacity to be unaffected by the intake. To some people the species is possibly better known as the 'yellow bird' in the Caribbean calypso song of the same name. (One wonders, incidentally, if the bananaquit's penchant for alcohol gave rise to a delicious-sounding cocktail called Yellow Bird that includes rum and crème de bananes.)

Alas the latest bottle-bank excursion produced rather sad evidence of a rodent's pleasure in red wine. What was probably a wood mouse had somehow squeezed through the 15-millimetre bottle neck but had then been too tipsy to find the exit. One can only hope that its passage into oblivion was softened by the cherry and vanilla notes of a rather good Rioja.

6 March 2018

Claxton, Norfolk

It is one of the more subtle attractions of our parish but its seasonal window is brief and upon us right now. It is composed of four very commonplace elements, but their convergence is as special and unpredictable as the arrival of a rare migrant.

It is the reflection of the reeds in the water, which doesn't sound very much but if conditions are perfect it is hypnotically beautiful. The reed has to be dead and bled entirely of any green hint so that it is pretty much the colour of African savanna. I often think of it as 'lion-flank beige'.

The second ingredient is a sky of winter sunshine so bright that the reflected water of Carleton Beck is ringing blue. Thirdly I need breeze, and preferably a south-westerly which carries the water towards the riverbank and its reed lining.

Yet any more than force 2–3 and the image is a clouded blue shattered by surface movement. Or the reflected colours of the reed ride only on surface ripples and one has a banded image that is pretty but conventional. Conversely, if there is too little breeze one gets an exact version of the reeds but upside down. There is momentary pleasure in these tricks of the light but they cannot sustain you.

What I need is for all these three elements to coalesce precisely. Then the reflected reed stems wander and deliquesce so that the surface vision ceases to have any similarity to its sources. If the reed lining is thick enough to exclude the reflected sky then it seems as if one is looking into a soon-setting reservoir of molten gold. Should sky and reed actually blend in the reflection then they acquire some of the appearance of Victorian marbled endpapers, or those globular, indefinable entities beloved of Salvador Dali: melted watches or whale-headed dreamers propped on poles.

The gold and blue interplay and fold suggestive forms into and upon themselves without end. Then I – for I am the fourth element – can share in the magic, impelled to try to capture it in words or photographs as the subliminal chromatic signature of this whole landscape.

## 7 March 2017

### ⤞ CLAXTON, NORFOLK ⤝

I am in heaven in recent days. Buckenham Marshes across the river is a mosaic of temporary splashes and mud-edged pools and, from the Yare's raised bank, I can see how it is smothered in late-winter pre-migration waders and wildfowl. All the flocking thousands are triggers, in turn, for the presence of many harriers and peregrines.

While the former circle continuously over the marsh, swinging and twisting in cold air, the peregrines are no more than ghosts spooking the others into wild free-ranging chaos. However, I did have one extraordinary sighting: on the evening of the new moon, a male and female peregrine spearing in tandem towards the southern horizon. Both closed their wings into a long stoop and they fell across the sky until I could see them only as two unequal-sized drops of mercury pulled by gravity into an ellipse.

Best of all are the churning masses that the peregrines leave in their wake. Wigeon boil up from the pools in fractal patterns and the white lines across the males' wings flash and re-flash in the grey waves of their panic. Thousands of lapwings are spread in smaller units across the marshes, but no matter how intense their own anxieties, lapwings can only look elegant. Lines of them slowly lilt and buckle in the sky and when each bird comes back down quietly to land its wings close over its white body like a black shutter. There was one remarkable moment I noticed when the stolid swans were utterly oblivious and head-down feeding but overhead a great rush of starlings passed and brushed up into their midst dunlins and ruffs, until all these birds were promiscuously globed together in one flock of fear.

It is extraordinary stuff and afterwards I head home with my brain full of it. I can sense all the exact sounds and sights sloshing out even as I rush down the beck, through the gate, up the glade, past the houses, to the front door. By the time I click the computer and press the first keys there is so little left of all that cold wind and wild bird blood except, perhaps, just enough for one short prayer.


15 March 2016

CLAXTON, NORFOLK

My guess is that on most days in the last 5,000 years buzzards have been commonplace over our village. Yet such was the relatively recent persecution of them by pheasant-killing folk that until 1994

I had never seen one at all in Norfolk. And it was only this century that I found them breeding locally. Now I spot them routinely from the office and ten during a walk on the marsh is nothing exceptional. However, I prefer to look upon the common buzzard as a rightful returnee, rather than a recently arrived stranger.

They look so at home, bulked upright on posts or squatting on the ground, where the bird's centre of gravity is across that bustling barrel chest. Even the deep brown of the plumage somehow looks old, and weathered like the local soil, which is not surprising given that buzzards often eat earth in the form of worms.

They are rooted creatures and not above humble fare including insects (beetles and moth larvae), frogs, snakes and even berries. Yet their reputation was long exaggerated. In the 1960s there were even shrill newspaper headlines that accused buzzards of eyeing up the infant contents of prams. Gamekeepers still illegally persecute them and in 2014 one Norfolk diehard was convicted after being caught with nine buzzards that he had poisoned.

The aerial bird has several personalities. Of all comparably sized raptors they have the shortest wings, mere paddles to drub the breeze. In level flight they can look awkward and laboured as if the wing beats cannot quite deliver the lift required by their bulk. At other times they sit on treetops and with each gust the wing feathers spread, then re-close, and spread again, as if the birds are so light and full of air they might be lifted upwards like a leaf into the wind. In truth they are in complete control. When the clouds clear and the sun emerges, buzzards rise to display in wide spirals and their calls spread across Claxton and all that blue heaven is distilled to a bird's single far cry.

19 March 2013

⤙ CLAXTON, NORFOLK ⤚

A week ago I was anticipating spring and the marshes were all winter-dried grasses — a place of owls, deer, vole runs and lark

song. Two full days of rain and now it's all changed. The fields
have become a 40-acre sheet of sparkling shallows – a site for
duck, migrant waders, gull cries and, for the first time this year,
the faintest hint of toad song.

It is steeped in sunlight, yet an acid northerly washes all
the air in the valley so that it is stripped of any possible heat
or comfort. Instead the landscape is bathed in cold brilliance
and I notice in some dykes there is still a surface crust of frost.
Over the entire expanse of water are black-headed gulls, many of
them now with the telltale chocolate hoods of breeding plumage.
The birds create the soundtrack for this new place and sustain a
perpetual gruff wavering laughter with an undertow of query or
surprise in the collective voice. Their movements are immensely
buoyant, a white blade on each forewing glinting like mica in
the sun. The deep beats create a pace that is adjusted perfectly
to the speed of the wind so that neither are the birds blown
backwards nor do they advance forwards, but row slowly across
the same wet spot, as if a perpetual non-progress carried its own
mysterious rewards.

As I stand to take in the complex wetland scene I realise
that it is as mutable as its predecessor. To the north a great
hammerhead of cloud grinds south all blue and black at its
upper levels and to write I have to stand feet planted apart, back
hunched to the wind, the hail rattling loud on my down jacket.
Then as quickly as it came, the squall is swept on and behind
come heavens of dancing blue. The sun returns. Every now and
then the gusts die, just momentarily the air thickens and there is
the slightest promise of something warmer.


20 March 2018

⊸ CLAXTON, NORFOLK ⊷

Even now there are several roadside heaps of it where the
snowdrifts had been so high that we were entirely cut off for

three days. These vestiges hardly conjure the power of that extraordinary storm, but it was fascinating to track the whole system as a single organism right down to its final details.

The most notable thing about 'the beast from the east' was the speed of its evolution. For example, on the morning it left it was astonishing how the natural world responded. Suddenly there were life sounds everywhere – starlings or greenfinches singing, a woodpecker drumming and sparrows re-immersed in their hedgerow palaver as if nothing had ever happened.

The snow that morning was entirely different. Every step raised a cleat-pressed pancake that snapped mid-point as it fell back into the footprint. The going was heavy and so unlike the snow at the height of the storm, when you could walk through it as if it were water. That virgin stuff was so loose it had blown deep into the heart of the vegetation and created a landscape so monochromatic that it was hard to distinguish photographs taken in black-and-white from those in colour.

On the marsh itself I experienced one of the rare occasions in lowland England where I thought: 'You could die out here.' The cold from the wind and horizontal snow left burning sensations at your temple and cheeks. Nothing stirred and the only warm-blooded life I saw, two swans midfield, were just curvatures of white enfolded in whiteness.

The storm's most powerful effect was its silence. The whole world became a sound-proofed closet, but for the relentless static from the easterlies and the faint-scratched footprint of every new flake. This atmosphere, however, triggered its own emotional impacts, for out of it, at one point, swung a lone blackbird, over the gate and into the boundary oaks, until its passage was obliterated by white. To see that bird, to know it was still here – that little feathered dinosaur, inheritor of the Jurassic, bringer of spring, announcer of dawn – among all that whitened silence, was as comforting as a flame in the dark.

## 21 March 2017

### ⨪ Claxton, Norfolk ⨪

I can surmise what a friend means when she says that part of the charm of lapwings is they look silly. It's the ridiculous crest, the unnecessary breadth of wing, which gives them so much more aerial lift and loop than they require, and then there is the zaniness of the spring display. Nor should we leave out the high-pitched notes that pass for song and which remind me of a dog's squeaky play bone wheezing in and out of tune as the animal chews.

Yet lapwings are too engrained in a lifetime of memory for me to think them only silly. They are the first sounds I awakened to as a naturalist in Derbyshire, whose nests we came upon in the grass like a revelation, and whose blotched-brown Easter eggs seemed a kind of miracle. Lapwing song was the omnipresent soundtrack of all my childhood springs. Now it has gone from behind our family home, as have 65 per cent of all Britain's lapwings since the 1970s. Their inexorable leave-taking has been central to that wider sense of wildlife loss throughout my adult life as an environmentalist, which includes forty-four million breeding birds.

Today as I watch thirty males song-flighting across the river, over the RSPB's Buckenham Marshes, I can forget briefly that lapwing is classified as near-threatened with global extinction. Males yo-yo everywhere you look, the squeezed-bone song arcing through the milky light of March and filling the valley with joy. Funny, really, to imagine, since all lapwings are is processed invertebrates, that this whole thing – the wing-thrum, the creaking cries, the blazing black-and-white rhyming of their wings – is just soil turned to song and dance.

I forget in which book, but the author W. H. Hudson suggests that beauty in nature is more important than beauty in art because, while we can go on filling galleries and museums with our works, once the life has gone from a place or species it is gone for ever. All I know is that as I get older I know with increased certainty that no book or even music triggers the same perennial flower of feeling as lapwings in display.

## 22 March 2014

### ❧ Claxton, Norfolk ❧

It was a source of wry amusement recently when a friend told me about the rook-scaring devices he'd seen in north Norfolk this spring. In fact you've probably seen them yourselves: lines of poles erected through a newly sown crop and from the top of each stick hangs a slaughtered corvid fluttering in the breeze.

My friend's observations illustrate the actual usefulness of the method, because the feeding birds were oblivious to the dead relative and at times were perched virtually on top of it. What crow sticks perhaps best indicate is not the intelligence of the species that uses them, but of their intended victim. There's no fooling a rook.

Most landowners at least acknowledge that much. I doubt there is a Norfolk farmer who wouldn't tell you how the birds can distinguish shotgun from stick at half a mile's range. Another good example of their ability to avoid persecution is the rooks' penchant for nesting in trees that overhang a busy road. Close to our home there are rookeries like this in the villages of Brooke and Bramerton.

Another classic strategy is to site the colony exactly where the birds' traditional persecutors are most numerous – right in the middle of town. Bungay, Beccles and Acle are all blessed in this way and it suggests an avian psychology similar to that expressed in the scene from *Godfather 2* when Michael Corleone recalls the words of his father Vito: 'Keep your friends close, but your enemies closer.' Rooks somehow know that they are safest in urban or domesticated environments where firearms are either illegal or too dangerous to be used.

Another expression of this family's brain power is the feat of memory involved in their food-caching behaviour. During the autumn a number of species including the European jay bury thousands of seeds in preparation for winter shortages. The British bird specialises in hiding about 5,000 acorns per autumn, but the nutcracker of northern Eurasia creates a larder containing as many as 100,000 various pine- and hazelnuts.

The birds have extraordinary abilities to remember the whereabouts of their secret stores but, of course, not all are retrieved. In fact such is the tree-planting and forest-tending behaviour of crows that even people who dislike them should at least have respect for the way the birds are husbanding our boreal forests in their slow climate-change-driven movement towards the north.

All of the above behaviour suggests how this family possesses quick wits, but a Cambridge-based academic, Professor Nicky Clayton, has now undertaken a series of experiments which demonstrate that crows are among the most intelligent avian families on Earth. The birds she uses belong to an American food-storing species called the scrub jay. In some experiments Clayton and her team gave them foods that either could be stored for long periods (peanuts) or would quickly perish (waxworms).

When the birds retrieved these items their behaviour varied according to the amount of time that had elapsed since the food was first hidden. When they were allowed to search just four hours after initial burial, the scrub jays retrieved their favourite food, the waxworms. However when the interval was raised to 124 hours the birds consistently searched only for the food that would still be in a state fit to consume – i.e. the peanuts. In short the birds remembered not just what and where they had buried the food, but also if it was worth recovering.

In the wild corvids often face the possibility of members of their own species observing their hard work and later stealing the stores they've hidden. It is assumed that a third of all wild larders are lost in this way. In another experiment Clayton's team allowed scrub jays to hide their food either when unobserved or when in the presence of another bird. In the latter scenario the scrub jay was much more likely, once left in private, to dig up the original cache and re-bury it at a new location. Another experiment showed how experienced birds – i.e. those that have previously stolen the stores of their neighbours – were much more likely to re-hide their caches than were naïve birds that had had no experience of pilfering. In short it required a bird to be a thief before it understood the possibility of falling victim to theft.

Based on her long-term studies Clayton suggests crows possess a cognitive toolkit that shows flexibility and imagination and combines abilities both to reason and to look ahead. These attributes suggest that the birds have an intelligence level similar to chimpanzees and they raise interesting questions about our treatment of the family.

It is widely felt that the intelligence and emotional complexity demonstrated by primates such as chimpanzees means that they should be elevated in our considerations and perhaps accorded basic 'animal rights'. It is argued that to kill or harm such a highly developed animal is a more morally loaded act than the slaughter, say, of something less evolved like an antelope or deer. However, Clayton's extraordinary revelations add challenging elements to the debate. If crows really are among our closest neighbours in terms of cognitive powers, then should we resort so readily to capital punishment whenever we judge them guilty of some agricultural infraction?

### 31 March 2014

#### ✒ BLACKWATER CARR, NORFOLK ✑

'The Lord spake unto Moses, Go unto Pharaoh, and say unto him, Let my people go. And if thou refuse to let them go, behold, I will smite all thy borders with frogs.' I just wished He would

plague my borders with frogs! I have more than 600 metres of
dyke along the edge of my patch, where neither a single frog's
leg nor the chirrup from a toad's sore throat has been seen or
heard for probably thirty years. Over that period the ditches had
become steadily overgrown by trees, clogged with their leaves
and deprived of oxygen. Yet for more than eighteen months I
have been trying to rehabilitate one length of dyke and restore
it to a condition fit for breeding amphibians. I then scoured the
neighbourhood for frogspawn with mixed success.

It seems a perfect measure of our upside-down environment
that not one site in my country parish, nor those of my friends,
has yielded the kind of froggy superabundance that might license
a little judicious redistribution. The most productive places were
all inner-city ponds, one of them so swollen with spawn that its
entire surface seemed topped by jelly. As the dusk blackbirds
sang, its owner described how, on one occasion, she'd counted
fifty smiling faces all raised from the pond's waterline.

I couldn't see much in the evening gloom but as I placed
each cold slithering handful into my bucket I could detect how
the spawn was already watery and loose, while those polka dots
of black life were elongated and almost animate. I stored them
in the garage overnight and when I went the following morning
to take them to Blackwater the upper third of the bucket was a
squirmy blur of dark blobs, tailed with diaphanous brown and
pocked by green pondweed and oxygen bubbles like frogs'-eyes.
As I poured this exquisite and suggestive soup into my dyke it
felt in more ways than one like an experiment in living.


## 31 March 2015

### ✄ Claxton, Norfolk ✄

All owls somehow make plainer the magic of life, but for me
short-eared owls cast the strongest spell, because they are part
of the story of how I became a naturalist. The birds bred on

Derbyshire moors near our house and each April evening after school I'd go and lie in the heather and be amazed at their displays. Owls in flight seem to love the air more truly than other birds. Each wing stroke is a perfect thing and short-eareds have longer wings than their four British relatives, so when they display all of this purity of movement is slowed and intensified to a form of aerial ballet.

The four birds at Claxton are only hunting before they return to breed in places like my home county. The voles on our marsh seem in good supply but the owls don't always get to keep their prey. One bird dropped as if on a catch and while I with binoculars couldn't see whether success had occurred or not, a kestrel clearly had. It flew low and hard at the owl's spot, paused, issuing an urgent whinnying cry, and flushed the owl out. A vole was visible in the talons and its owner began a steady circling ascent over the kestrel, which maintained its pursuit.

It must have been five minutes before I witnessed the outcome and willed it because of the pain in my arms from holding binoculars. Up they went, higher and higher, the owl even seeming to place its broad span over its opponent to block that bird's upward spiral. The owl then tried vainly to scoop the meat from foot to beak but that failed. Still they rose until each bird was no more than a dot and the kestrel's relentless shrieks were all but lost in all that vast air. Then the end came. The vole was dropped and in a second the dot-sized assailant caught the speck. The kestrel's wings now closed and their owner fell to Earth at an angle to it of about 70 degrees. Just before the dark teardrop splashed, miraculously and without apparent adjustment, it stopped and landed and vanished.

# APRIL

1 April 2013

The water vole was so much a part of my Derbyshire childhood on the banks of the River Wye that I find it almost painful now to recall, given its present catastrophic decline, with what indifference I once viewed this glorious little mammal. Yet in the 1970s it was everywhere.

We would stop at almost any point along the Wye – to scrutinise a dabchick, dipper or grey wagtail – and there overlooked at the edge of the tableau, so to speak, was the birds' gentle riverine neighbour. Water voles always looked supremely rotund and, wrapped in that gorgeous waterproof fur, they somehow seemed to possess a proprietorial insouciance as if they felt assured of their lifelong tenancy on the mud banks of this famous trout stream.

Invariably the creature's jowls bulged and the jaws, with those extraordinary orange incisors, were grinding nonchalantly on some waterside vegetation. Our mutual disregard was perhaps rooted in an assumption that things would always be so. How wrong I was.

What does it mean to lose connection with such a marginal part of our lives? Perhaps nothing we can put a price on will be forfeit. No bank will fail, no house will fall, no human child starve. Yet we should all recognise that with the passing of another fixture from our natural world we suffer a major defeat. We have lost some of the delicacy, the intricate textured richness, that is the very stuff of life and of lived experience.

Should any of you doubt it, then imagine a childhood without Kenneth Grahame's *Wind in the Willows*. I read it in my youth and more recently read it aloud to my girls. Yet its central character 'Ratty', the anxious rodent with that genius for friendship and for rowing boats and for picnics by the passing stream, is none other than our own *Arvicola amphibius*. If there are no water voles in our landscapes then there will certainly be none to fill the dreams and the stories of our childhood. When we have no water voles we lose one more way of imagining our place in the world.

I have very occasionally seen the real creature here in my Norfolk patch, but the encounters come with a macabre twist. Our surviving population, which has to contend with those predatory mink, has become as cautious and wary as its Derbyshire cousins were once bold. So in twelve years I've never once stumbled upon that casual scene played out on the Wye. In fact I've needed eyes and appetites far more acute than my own simply to see them: both of my sightings have involved the poor vole being shovelled down into the capacious gullet of a hunting heron.

This spring's encounter was even more dramatic. I had gone to photograph an obliging otter on Norfolk's River Thet and in the final moments of that session the creature gave chase to a water vole. Hunter and hunted squirmed and twisted through the riverside weed then up the bank in increasing desperation. With my camera I machine-gunned those moments like any paparazzo after a princess. Later, unpicking the images one by one, I pieced together the story that I'd witnessed. And this one has a happy ending. Ratty lived to row his boat another day.

2 April 2015

❧ CLAXTON, NORFOLK ❧

I vividly recall the Cromer-born environmental activist and filmmaker, the late Tony Hare, remarking once that he always judged a book by its cover. It was a typically humorous comment by this immensely talented man, but it also contained an essential truth.

Even in an age of digital downloads the art of the book cover is still a fundamental part of publishing. However disembodied the product may become, there still needs to be some summarising image that encapsulates the contents and which can be used on all kinds of publicity. And if that single visual motif fails to connect with the audience then the book will struggle.

This is where the genius of Jonathan Gibbs (www. jonathangibbs.com) comes into play. A superb exhibition, entitled 'Life is but a Dream', features a selection of his most recent book illustrations and runs until 30 April at the Corn Hall Gallery in Diss.

As well as being an acclaimed artist in his own right, Jonathan is the long-established head of illustration at the prestigious Edinburgh College of Art. He may spend much of his life in the Scottish capital but outside term time Jonathan is a regular in our region because his parents still live near Beccles. He was also East Anglian born and reared, having attended Lowestoft School of Art to complete his foundation course. From there he progressed to the Central School of Art in London and then spent another two years at the Slade School of Fine Art.

Jonathan's abstract landscape paintings, many of them in oil, pastel or crayon, reflect his deep sensitivity to line and architectural shape in natural objects or land formations. Some of this he traces back to the formative influence of our own regional countryside, which is so dominated by linear horizons, flat planes of colour in the water or the sky and by the rectilinear patterns that are created by the structure of Norfolk's hedges, or through the incidental operations of the farmer's plough.

However the art form that Jonathan has truly made his own is wood engraving and it is this technique that is used in his wonderful book covers and illustrations. Unlike typical prints, which are created by cutting into the softer side grain of a wood block, engraving entails using the much more resistant end grain.

The material might be more challenging, but the results tend to be correspondingly richer. The strength of the wood allows the print to carry more intricate detail and a small image can convey huge amounts of information.

The wildlife illustrator Thomas Bewick was an early exponent and populariser of the method and Jonathan cites the eighteenth-century artist as one of his influences. Yet he also has an enduring fascination with the works of Matisse, Bonnard and Picasso, as well as the twentieth-century English war painter Paul Nash.

One of the things that strikes me about Jonathan Gibbs's work is the ability to create an enormous sense of geographical space within what can seem a small, even cramped two-dimensional area. Equally one sees his self-declared love of geometric and recurring linear patterns in his own art, but there is always a corresponding sensitivity to the flowing, liquid qualities of wild creatures or to the elastic shapes of foliage and trees.

I am always astounded by the way that an artist like Jonathan Gibbs can take the original germ of an idea for an illustration then turn it into something concrete and beautiful. I must confess, I know a little of this process because he has now done three of the images for my own books. On each occasion I am struck by the aptness of the art to the written contents.

None has been more affecting than his transformation of my initial concept for a cover on *Claxton: Field Notes from a Small Planet.* I recall telling Jonathan of a strange occasion one winter's evening, when a white icy mist hung over the fields and the frost lined all the vegetation down the dyke. At the very split second that I took a photograph of these details an owl passed by and I caught the reflection of it – but not the creature itself – in the water as it flew.

I thought this scene was a way to convey the notion that the book was a reflection of landscape and a recreation of special moments that I had encountered in it. Jonathan's subsequent engraving caught that strange vision of the owl's mirror image, but it also encapsulated something about all Norfolk landscapes.

When you pick up a book it is so easy to overlook the process by which the physical object is constructed and easier still to give no thought whatsoever to what is, in effect, the most important page of all: the one that enfolds the cover. For once the exhibition at the Diss Corn Hall allows us to celebrate this quiet art form and to recognise the immense, if unassuming, talent that it requires.

## 4 April 2017

### BUXTON, DERBYSHIRE

What is it about frogs and toads that has made them such classic icons of sexual reproduction? It cannot be timing because their breeding is often over before the other elements of high spring – flowers, bees, birdsong, warm temperatures – are in full flood. Frogs will gather at the spawning pond when the starlit nights are frosted and the vegetation rimed in white.

Nor can it be that frogs or toads flesh out the dawn chorus. I have often found that frogs are most vocal on late winter nights and the minuscule burp of toads, which is more creak than croak, is so quiet one has to strain to pick it out. The soft even purring of frogs is sweeter but a herpetologist noted that a pondful of thousands in full throat was completely inaudible just 50 metres away.

One aspect must surely be the volume of their fertilised eggs not to mention their richly suggestive physical form. When I was a child I loved to run my hands through the pond water to get the strange claggy jelliness of it. Here at Lightwood, less than 1 kilometre from where I was born, the frogs' reproductive labours have been prodigious. There's one immense reef of spawn and when I spotted a lone toad doing a breaststroke through it, the old man's legs sculling in perfect synchrony, it reminded me a little of a bird passing through dark cloud.

I suspect what really compels our imaginations is their sheer drive. Toads climb walls to get to spawning ponds. They will arrive already atop their mates, glued to her with a grip known as amplexus. He can keep it up for weeks and not even taking away his head loosens his ardour. She, meanwhile, can become englobed in testosterone, twelve males smothering her even until she drowns and starts to decompose. They do this, without fail, year upon year. By coincidence I find that on exactly this date thirty-three years ago I was on this same spot looking at frogs and I guess that the ones I see now are related to those once enjoyed by my former self.

## 14 April 2014

### MAY DAY FARM, SUFFOLK

Thetford Forest runs for at least 15 miles from the Norfolk village of Munford to Suffolk's River Lark and must be one of the largest timber plantations in southern England. You can walk and walk and experience nothing but conifer block after block, made more monotonous by the gentle tilt of the ground and the confusing rectilinear grid of firebreaks. Yet in this place of sameness we came upon an extraordinarily particularised moment.

With its straddle of wooden buildings and the pleasing muddle of its garden, the dwelling called Shaker's Lodge seemed an unexpected fragment of human wilderness hidden among all this marching and militarised nature. And there on the shingle path by its gate was a small puddle to which hundreds of bright birds poured down like fallen blossom.

They were finches come to drink and dominated by bramblings, a cold-weather migrant that arrives from boreal Scandinavia. The male's breast is suffused with the exact orange of the winter sun at dusk. His back is a complex interlacing of dark and light shades ('brambling' is thought to derive from 'brandling', an old word for various animals with this pattern). He has the distinction in spring of a solidly black head that is acquired by the gradual rubbing away of frosted white tips to each feather. Come April he is a magnificent two-tone beauty and I know people for whom it is a favourite bird.

Yet the song is one of those rudimentary non-songs, a weird aspirant monosyllable, a brief rattle of metal or the rubbing together of something hard. Here, each song from a hundred birds overlapped with its neighbour's until it seemed, as my companion so aptly put it, as if the whole wood were wheezing. Then there were the nasal chattering sounds of redpolls, the rubbery fizz of siskins and the precise soft chip calls of crossbills. They formed a glorious cacophony of mechanical notes, a dry music from which all possible moisture had been squeezed and a unique spring chorus but played out on winter's instruments.

## 16 April 2012

### ⤛ Ridgehead Farm, Staffordshire ⤜

A snipe in full display is one of the strangest birds of the air you could hope to see. That striped earth-brown body that makes this wader almost impossible to spot on the ground is suddenly flung up like a mud pie to the heavens. The wings flicker in quick shallow beats almost like a skylark's in mid-song and it could even be a lark except for that extraordinary wand-like bill poking ahead of him. This weirdly disproportionate silhouette then careers in a series of fluttering ascents and even steeper descents and performs an invisible crown-shaped circuit across the skies. As he goes he creates two interlocking sounds. The background note is vocal – a constant *chikk-a, chikk-a, chikk-a* – but to each of its daredevil dives it adds a long-drawn shuddering sound that is mysterious and arresting.

Our forebears were bamboozled by it. They called this bird the horse gokk or, in Gaelic, *gabharin reo*, 'little goat of the frost', to suggest the sound's similarity to neighing or bleating livestock. They also made it a portent of thunder or rain, and, in fact, snipe often perform amid April showers. Yet the truth of that strange note was not revealed until the early twentieth century in one of the unlikeliest of settings. Pagani's in Edwardian London was described as a 'somewhat sleazy Italian restaurant where even the waiters' coats were stained with grease'. Amid the soiled linen and abominable food, an ornithologist, Philip Manson-Bahr, unfolded to the assembled members of the British Ornithologists' Club the mysteries of a snipe's love song. He proceeded to whirl around the restaurant a cork on a long string, to which he had fixed a snipe's outer-tail feathers, and with this strange contrivance he reproduced the bird's breathy song. Today my wonderful binoculars allow me to see, when this bird dives overhead, the same hard pin-like feathers vibrating even as the shuddering woodwind music is produced.

## 17 April 2018

### ⟞ CLAXTON, NORFOLK ⟝

This spring I've been amused by our wild violets that have spread suddenly across one half of the lawn. For anyone who has never met them, they are an absolute joy. Each flowering spike bears an asymmetrical corolla that comprises five petals of the most intense purple. Down the throat of the central spur is a delicious little nectary that bees apparently find irresistible.

If I crouch to sniff it also yields this gentle odour, from which I judge them to be sweet violets, *Viola odorata*, the one common species in the family that has such a scent. It is highly evocative, bringing to mind my childhood when we used to buy those tubes of purplish sugar known as Parma Violets. (They were, in fact, a Derbyshire speciality manufactured in New Mills.)

I'm amused by the plants, but also instructed, because while their spread suggests a hint of drama, I am sure that suddenness has nothing to do with it. What is more likely is that some years ago an original pioneer took root and then sent out rhizomes to creep inch-wise across our lawn bank. In fact, I recall registering a violet or two last year and took pictures to celebrate the 'arrival'.

This spring the colony has expanded its territory to the extent that there are now 146 flowers in total. Yet the whole process represents ten years' patient work and the key lesson is not that the flowers themselves have done anything in a rush, rather it is I – my awareness – that has changed overnight.

There is a second major flaw in my account of our violets, namely that they are in any way to do with us. In truth, they came without asking. They spread without assistance. They flourished without notice. And it is conceivable that they could die out without me being able to do anything to prevent it. Our only part in the transaction, which has blessed our garden with glorious colour, is to have done nothing: not cut, not sprayed, not worried, not intervened and not mown, but once. And that, in most gardening, appears to be the hardest thing of all.


## 19 April 2016

### ⤙ LIGHTWOOD, DERBYSHIRE ⤚

Compare the old and new maps of this part of Buxton and you'll notice how the valley's wedge-shaped block of blue has morphed into a line threaded through several blue specks. Those cartographic changes reflect a heart-warming story of how toads can alter whole landscapes.

The wedge-shaped block was once a reservoir and when it was decommissioned by Severn Trent, the company was highly sensitive to local wishes that Lightwood's wildlife should be accommodated. The map's blue spots now mark the presence of three wonderful ponds that ensure the survival of its toads and frogs.

This morning toads are everywhere. While their relatives bred last month and left a great loll of frogspawn to swamp one entire bay of the pool, the toads are just arriving. One woman we met spoke of thousands trooping towards it last week. At any moment there are scores bubbled up at the surface, their copper eyes flaring among the forests of water mint.

Toad sex is a weird ferment of life and death. The females, which are huge compared with their multiple mates, act like magnets for all that testosterone. Soon she's entirely smothered in male flesh so that they writhe as a single mud globe. Sometimes they sink to the bottom and routinely she's drowned. We spotted several females, all spread-eagled and upside-down and ghostly angel-white in the murk.

Eventually we became connoisseurs of these mating masses: an orgy of four to five toads together were little more than embryonic; a bolus of eight might hold us briefly, but the real toad ball numbered about a dozen. These miniature planets of flesh revolved like some strange inkblot test that lured scattergun associations from us: out popped Aristophanes, then Thoreau's *Walden*, Richard Kerridge's *Cold Blood*. The sad wide-mouthed smiles of the males had a hint of young croc or, at the other end of the spectrum, Charles Laughton's bulbous mug in *Hobson's Choice*. Toads are disgusting and mesmerising all at once, yet mingled with sunlight and thrush song and the flaring yellow bolts of coltsfoot spiking out of the Earth, they reassure us that life and Lightwood are good and all is exactly as it should be.

## 21 April 2015

### CLAXTON, NORFOLK

Every morning over the past few weeks and with the arrival of that ambiguous grey glow of dawn there comes to me the blended song from all of Claxton's blackbirds. As I lie listening to the daffodil freshness of it I try to separate out what makes their collective music so moving at such an early hour.

Is it the fact that in order to produce it, air must rush over each bird's syrinx, in and out, as it makes music but also as it breathes? That same stuff – basically two parts oxygen and eight parts nitrogen – serves as the medium bearing the sounds in waves across the garden and through the window to my ears. Yet it is also what I can hear passing in and out of me, as I lie listening to my blackbirds.

It is our air – and only our air – that lets blackbirds sing and brings the music to me and which the birds and I share with every living thing wrapped around the world. How extraordinary to think that, if I set out this dawn and could walk Spiderman-like up the sheer wall of this atmosphere, then within just three days of my departure I would reach the edge of its territory, in a layer we call the thermosphere. You would not find it after what is roughly the 120 kilometre marker. All beyond is just darkness and the dead music of the stars.

As a child they always led me to believe that heaven was somewhere up among all that nothing. Even now we should bear in mind, when next the astrophysicists bid us spend our billions venturing out into the dark vault of outer space, that the thing they really seek is all here coming out of the blackbirds' beaks.

Spiders have been recorded sailing their silk at an altitude of 5 kilometres, and penicillin spores were found flying at 77 kilometres, but most of the things we should value are in that infinitesimally thin air layer, perhaps 100 metres deep, where birdsong is best heard and where you and I usually sleep. I know now that there are no such things as angels, but were I ever allowed to name them, then all mine would be black with orange beaks.

## 28 April 2014

### ⤖ Langdon Beck, Upper Teesdale ⤛

As I look south-west towards the wonderfully named Cronkley Scar I am struck by the absolute weirdness of our everyday world:

by a tale so strange that I have no need of the supernatural to
make my Easter seem full of miracles. For the great wall-like
rampart of Cronkley, with its chaotic hem of boulder scree, is
comprised of Whin Sill, an igneous rock that rose towards the
Earth's surface 295 million years ago. As it boiled up the magma
extruded through faults in surrounding limestone layers until they
too were cooked and hardened in its molten inferno. (These are
now a coarse crystalline marble known by a beautifully expressive
oxymoron: sugar limestone.) What seems most wondrous is that
those sedimentary layers were, in turn, laid down forty million
years earlier, when this part of northern England lay over the
Equator.

Weirdest of all, perhaps, is that geologists have somehow
managed to unravel this story so that we too might marvel at
the way the seeming permanence of the place is really all in flux
through time and space.

It is not only the long odyssey of Cronkley that strikes
me, but also its vast presence in the living moment: the
cold updraughts it billows above the crest so that a fly-sized
buzzard hangs motionless. There are the subtle, soft-coloured
lichens that mottle the boulders right now and make of them
a kind of cartography. There is then the momentary sad music
of lapwings and curlews that are so abundant here – and
reminding me of Derbyshire forty years ago; this is the richest
landscape for breeding waders in all England. Most satisfying
are the migrant ring ouzels which, for now, forsake Cronkley's
wind-blasted summit and feed on aquatic flies on the banks
of the River Tees. There is a curious note of human poetry at
Cronkley – the television aerial extruding from a whitewashed
cottage wall by the dusty window with its soiled lace. No
doubt the device channels to this quintessential fragment of
Carboniferous England passing tales of Korea and the Ukraine
and South Sudan.

## 29 April 2013

### ⤐ CLAXTON, NORFOLK ⤏

The weather has been so unstintingly poor in the last few months that it seems almost perverse to wish for rain. Yet, in truth, we're in need yet again. On our allotment the upper soil layer is a boot's depth of mere powder. A friend also told me recently of local farmers who are paying the price for the clearance of all their hedges. Tonnes of topsoil were being ripped off some of the largest bare fields and sand-blasting everything that lay downwind.

If we need rain then this morning's downpour could not have been gentler nor more atmospheric. As I walk the lane to the marsh it dissolves and releases from the parched, grey crumbled ground that glorious earthy perfume that one catches best right at the back of the nose. It's not a particularly powerful odour. (I notice, by contrast, how on passing a spot where the fox has sprainted, I'm assailed by the vulpine stink as if I had been hit physically.) While the Earth's own scent may be far gentler it is both pervasive and unmistakable. Who knows what are its precise constituents but it's an odour I emphatically associate with asphalt and high summer and that moment when the queen black ants and their winged male attendants all pour out of the cracks in the pavements and take flight for the only time in their lives.

It also has a hint of the Mediterranean, especially of thistle-rich broken ground where one surmises that it is strongly linked to all those sun-baked spiny plants. Here at Claxton it has the same note of oil-based astringency and it wells up even thicker as the rain intensifies. What is initially just a mist of spreading concentric ripples on the dyke has become a rattling plop of sharp drops in water and clear bubbles like frog's eyes at the surface. The odour of spring swells up fatter and is sweetened now by the lemon blossom of sallows on the marsh.

# MAY

1 May 2018

It was wonderful as well as instructive to sit with Miriam, my younger daughter, at the edge of the wetland scrape that is the showcase of this RSPB reserve.

Here before us in lines that were as clear-cut as the grating calls of the 1,000 breeding gulls were godwits and plovers, curlews and spring's first swallow. Here were the sounds of shelduck and Cetti's warblers, redshank and sandpipers. Here were ruff in summer plumage, heads up and down, all feeding in sewing-machine mode while teal with shoveler dabbled in the shallows. All intermittently fed and flew, buzzed by a sparrowhawk or passing harrier, and a spreading arc of wings would swirl into the air and then, all of a sudden, they would plump back down as one and appear again as they had begun. It was the typical exhilarating stuff of spring at this spot – a perpetually renewed milky way of birds stretched across a marsh.

As we watched we also pondered the recent BBC television series *Civilisations*. Great, we said, that they had added to the dead white European men, who were the only constituents of Kenneth Clark's original *Civilisation* series. The presenters Mary Beard and David Olusoga add diversity to the mix, yet the essential fixture is still apparent. We seem unable to escape or rise above the idea that civilisation is things – paintings, sculptures, buildings, art. The Canadian ecologist John Livingston once lamented that 'our sundry aesthetic models' have no place for living processes and that 'our culture is essentially abiotic' – i.e. lifeless.

We recalled the TV programme's images of Simon Schama amid the ecstatic effects of Chartres Cathedral and wondered whether Titchwell too — here, now — wasn't also a kind of cathedral, an endlessly renewed scene of biodiversity and beauty made by sunlight and fashioned from stardust. In the same spring that we saw the last male northern white rhinoceros, that giraffes were declared at risk of extinction and one in eight of the world's 10,000 species were judged to be similarly imperilled, do we not need to visit the whole idea of civilisation once more?

## 3 May 2016

### ⤳ CLAXTON, NORFOLK ⤶

Normally all the softness of the English summer is in a blackbird's syrinx. Today, however, as the sound of the song wafts towards me across the garden it somehow seems to congeal in these north-easterlies. It is like a dark warm spawn-filled pond of music but with ice edges. I go out and the air is cold. The new greens in the hawthorn and the oaks are cold in tone. Even the sunlight feels cold and the blue above has clouds with an unmistakable hint of snow.

Sure enough, when it rains for about sixty seconds as I reach the marsh, it falls as hail. Then it stops again. The sun beats down and it feels like the weirdest spring I can recall.

Yet none of it appears to bother the water lilies. Their leaves are coming up everywhere and I am intrigued at the way in which they settle at the surface as waxed plates of emerald but rise through the water column of the beck as crinkled fronds of lettuce green. All that vegetable luxuriance wafting in fluid looks so inviting but if I stuck my bare feet in the mulch from which it emerges, I know that they would be numb in seconds.

The one feature of my walk that has no seasonal ambiguity is the territorial behaviour of the peacock butterflies. Asleep for five months and fuelled winter-long by last autumn's blackberries, the butterflies have wings thinner than lily petals and coated in burgundy plush with four owl's-eye spots. They love this nettle-rich stretch all the way along the bank of the beck and as I walk down they rise up at intervals in territorial flights – two insects, both males, thrusting up in momentary columns of furious combat. To be touched by those fluttering wings is to be brushed by velvet. Yet in this way they contest anything that transgresses their boundary: other peacocks, small tortoiseshells, one even chased a sedge warbler. The book tells me that they will react aggressively to thrown clods of earth. No cold unseasonal breeze can halt a peacock's passion.

## 5 May 2015

### ⟶ Loch Shurrery, Caithness ⟵

As I walked south from Shurrery Lodge into this classic plain of Flow Country I struggled to define the exact nature of its impact. Yes, it was big, perhaps the biggest British landscape I've ever seen. In fact it took a while to work out that the cone-shaped peak looming over all the day's experiences wasn't even on the same OS sheet as me. It was Ben Griam Beg, at least 30 kilometres away.

It wasn't just size: it was scale combined with its levelness and its uniformity of colour. The problem with this assertion is that it suggests something samey or bland, when the place is everything but. The primary note is the brown of heather that is always, depending on sunlight or cloud, edging back and forth out of purple. Into this vast plane of sameness was inserted the silver shards from a hundred dubh lochans, fragmented pools that shimmer at the bog's surface. Then surrounding all the day in a form I have never previously encountered was its silence.

Silence so deep it had a plastic tangible presence. It filled in behind and around the music of skylarks or curlews or golden plovers, or, at times, simply the breeze, like a membrane.

Everything was blanketed in clarity. It was only days later when I went south that I understood how far the white noise of life had been obliterated in that place.

How strange to reflect that at the end of last century we sought to ruin the Flows. The story makes a strange environmental riddle. Which banana republic would seek to destroy the one rare habitat of which it held the world's largest portion, in order to give tax breaks to the very wealthy to grow low-grade timber? The answer was the British government of the mid eighties. International pressure eventually told, but not before Rifkind and Ridley had taken their moiety of revenge. By breaking apart the Nature Conservancy Council they effectively ended the post-war project of state conservation. In the Flows the past is omnipresent. Its silence lets you summon the mist procession and all its clamorous ghosts as if they were yesterday.

## 12 May 2014

### ❥ Blackwater Carr, Norfolk ❧

Last night a friend told me that if he could live all his life in a single month then it would have to be May. Most naturalists would say Amen to that. It's the way things suddenly loosen, become freer; in J. A. Baker's memorable phrase, the air itself is suddenly 'without edges'. Then there's the magical injection of colour and always the sharp sense of anticipation at reacquiring old companions. Finally there are the details – the life-affirming tide of song each dawn, the bumblebees truffling in deadnettle and at dusk the smoke wisps of invertebrates through and above the sallows.

It's odd how these aerial dance formations of nameless insects awaken so little in most people – indifference at best, at worst shivers of disgust. Collectively humanity will spend somewhere around $45 billion on chemical pesticides this year. Yet that vast efflorescence of insect life is integral to spring. After all, those swifts newly screaming over our village and the chorus that greets us at first light are little more than arthropods processed by avian digestive systems. Even the nightingale's exquisite music, hoped for but, as yet, unheard by the Yare this May, is just invertebrate mash converted to energy and deployed in the bird's heaven-sent syrinx.

Think of it this way: spring simply as one vast insect garden, an immense enveloping mystery of winged life – perhaps a million such creatures within a 100-metre radius every moment of our own May lives. This week I plucked a single distinct bloom from this invertebrate garden and was amazed. It was a tiny pollen-eating moth called the black-headed gold. Its wings formed a soft-fringed tent of sparkling colour which, according to the light, shone in bands of bronze-green and reddish gold. There have possibly been as few as a dozen records in East Anglia since 1859, although these may reflect the infrequency of our encounters, rather than genuine scarcity. There it was as bright as brass on a bramble leaf, until this fragment of spring spiralled off into May's wider invertebrate mysteries.

## 15 May 2016

### ❧ CLAXTON, NORFOLK ❧

In Cormac McCarthy's *The Road*, his tale of human survival in a post-apocalyptic world, there is a very tender moment when he describes one of the book's only two characters, known simply as 'the man', waking at night from his dreams. He emerges, McCarthy writes, 'in the black and freezing waste out of softly colored worlds of human love, the songs of birds, the sun'.

In a landscape of man-made death who wouldn't dream of the sun and human love? Where would we be without them? Their place among the rock-bottom necessities of life is really a given. But birdsong? Why exactly is that part of the trio?

Yet responses to the sounds of birds are deeply embedded in almost all human cultures. My guess is if you searched for the most commonly recurring natural motif, not just in all European, but in all Arabic and Persian poetry, you'd find nightingale song a strong contender for first place. But why exactly do we find them so arresting?

I think part of the answer lies in the sheer range and power of those sounds and these, in turn, are linked to the mechanics of the avian vocal organ, known as the syrinx. A complex of vibrating membranes, cartilage and muscle all within a resonating chamber, the syrinx is probably the most sophisticated creator of sound in all nature. Its versatility is almost limitless. Many of the noises it can produce are beyond our capacity to register, because they are either too high- or too low-pitched for the human ear.

Take a single species, an Australian songbird called the superb lyrebird, which is well known for its remarkable abilities to mimic other sounds. It can produce note-perfect renditions of car engines, camera motor-drives, petrol-driven chainsaws. It can conjure the combined effects of an entire flock of parrots. And not just the various vocalisations of the multiple birds, but even, and simultaneously, the physical noises created by the birds' plumage as it beats the air or brushes against foliage.

One of the most moving cases of lyrebird mimicry was what seemed like a human tune produced by several birds in the woods of New South Wales in the late 1960s. On investigation it turned out that forty years earlier someone had kept a tame lyrebird on a property nearby, and the owner had been accustomed to play to it a pair of Irish airs on his flute. The bird had learnt the songs, but then other wild lyrebirds nearby had picked up the motifs from their captive neighbour and incorporated Irish folk music into their own repertoires. Decades later, the lyrebird community still honoured those old tunes as part of their local song cycle.

Here is the extraordinary revelation about birds' vocal capabilities. The wild lyrebirds didn't recreate each human melody separately. The sophisticated nature of the avian syrinx meant that they were able to combine both in a single simultaneous performance, the two songs all at once.

That story touches upon another element that helps explain why the sounds of birds are so captivating to us. It is the way they are passed from bird to bird. Take, for instance, the song thrush, that glorious spot-chested inhabitant of East Anglian woodland that is among the first birds to sing in spring. The song has a bell-like, ringing, declarative quality. It is also loud and invincibly optimistic – an emphatic 'Yes!' on the issue of life's renewal. It is a bird that thinks all is for the best in the best of all possible worlds. (It is sad, then, to reflect that changed practices on our farms have caused the loss of half of all British song thrushes since the 1960s.)

Each bird you hear has learnt its repertoire of sounds from its near neighbours, and probably its own relatives. In effect, one song thrush generation passes on to the next a song torch peculiar to its species. What you are hearing, as you savour that first bird early in the new year, is not just the exquisite freshness of its performance. You are hearing all the song thrushes that have ever lived in your neighbourhood. You are blessed by a sound at once filled with a sense of the moment, but also latent with the past. Song-thrush song is far older than the idea of England, older than this island itself – a sound of the whole Holocene that has sailed over the heads of British woods since the last ice age. It is well-worn and venerable and completely new all at the same time.

Something of that latent reverberation in birdsong is celebrated in one of the most famous and beloved poems in the English language, a popularity, incidentally, that tells us a great deal about the universal impact of avian sounds. It is Edward Thomas's *Adlestrop*.

Yes, I remember Adlestrop –
The name, because one afternoon

Of heat the express-train drew up there
Unwontedly. It was late June.

The steam hissed. Someone cleared his throat.
No one left and no one came
On the bare platform. What I saw
Was Adlestrop – only the name

And willows, willow-herb, and grass,
And meadowsweet, and haycocks dry,
No whit less still and lonely fair
Than the high cloudlets in the sky.

And for that minute a blackbird sang
Close by, and round him, mistier,
Farther and farther, all the birds
Of Oxfordshire and Gloucestershire.

Thomas captures so perfectly that momentary insight we have
that their singing is not confined to our time and place. It is
expansive and even universal. My only question of Thomas is
why did you limit your sense of the birds' spreading net of music
to only two English counties?

One of the most powerful causal connections in birdsong
is the awakening impact of light. We call it the 'dawn chorus'
for a good reason. Every morning, for about three months
during spring, birds are prompted to make music as the light
returns. In our hemisphere, between approximately 30 and
60 degrees north, almost all songbirds are inspired by the
presence of our life-giving star and they pour forth wherever
they feel its touch.

What song is doing for the birds themselves is defining their
nesting areas and advertising their sexual fitness to breed. Each
separate territory forms a jigsaw piece interlocking with all its
neighbours. And this process of spatial division among birds

continues not just across biomes, but across whole continents. So song serves as a form of territorial warfare and a regulator of sexual politics, but conducted by music alone. It is, in every sense, a harmonising of each bird to its neighbours and to the Earth's resources.

In the light of these ideas I ask you to rethink, say, the blackbird in your garden, when it starts to create that gloriously mellow sound tomorrow morning. Blackbirds, since they are so common and widespread, sing everywhere and almost all at once. They transcend our arbitrary geographical and national divisions. Millions of them harness their voices to the sun. And each blackbird, including the one near you, is part of an empire of music.

All birds in our hemisphere do this. Of course there will be physical gaps in its daily journey around our planet. The Atlantic imposes its own unbridgeable silence on the song cycle. The music will gutter out as it hops, island to island, through the Aleutians. The icy waters of the Bering Strait will also douse it. But it revives on the Siberian shores and returns, a high-crested wave of distilled life that surges west through Eurasia and then America. Every year, probably for the last ten thousand, it has repeated the same pattern.

Bird vocalisations are integral to our sense experience and have been so since the origins of our species. Their song is a subliminal fixture in our collective story but also in the story of each of us as individuals. Birdsong thus becomes a way of measuring and narrating our lives. When I wrote of this once, a reader in the *Guardian* suggested we call it the 'songosphere'. What a wonderful name! What an idea: that blessed 100-metre-deep layer of air, wrapped right around the entire northern half of the planet like a warming scarf of sound, created by billions of voices.

So I bid you now: stop reading and put down this page, go outside and tune into the songosphere. And give thanks for the greatest song on Earth.

## 15 May 2018

### ⤜ AIGAS FIELD CENTRE, HIGHLANDS ⤛

For more than ninety minutes we had sat until cold air quieted the wood and the day thinned into the long shadows of the trees. By 10.30 p.m. we were centred in an arc of artificial lamp glow. There was just the sound of a last robin across the loch, whose spindly song was an analogue for the vanishing day.

The silent theatricality of the moment was thus complete when the creature strolled into our vision without the merest hint of drama. Its step was sprightly, its acceptance of the lamp instantaneous. It brought a touch of night in its sharp black muzzle and in the big silent dark-stockinged feet – and every now and then it paused from eating to stare hard at its own route through the trees, reassuring itself of solitude – but otherwise we were all at ease with the mutual encounter. For ten minutes there were no sounds except the crunch of nuts and the click of cameras.

This is the cold killer widely accused of wiping out the chicken coop in one night. This is the sure-footed predator who can race through the canopy to snatch a squirrel in full flight from a topmost twig. This is the invader well able to steal shadow-like into an occupied house and den in the attic. Yet the things I noticed most were the dewdrops beaded on its luxuriant fur, the pinkness of the pointed tongue, the relish with which those carnassials ground up peanuts. It could so easily have been someone's pet.

It snuffled under our gaze for each final morsel, it tricked along a birch beam to slurp at dribbles of honey. Its route back to ground was as careless and assured as the ascent and there was one extraordinary moment when its hind claws clipped it to a branch above and down the creature dangled as if in a harness of loose fur, as if it had momentarily forgotten those rear legs bound over its head, as if gravity were just another plaything. It extracted a last dewdrop of sweetness. Then without sound, without more ado, it vanished and we were alone with the silent thrill of a pine marten.

## 16 May 2017

### ⤳ Buxton, Derbyshire ⤳

After the most rainless spring that I can recall, the vegetation on the moor tops is frazzled to an August tinder. The full sweep of folded slopes looks grey rather than the usual heathery brown and even the deepest gullies are dry bottomed and crunchy underfoot. Yet the strong north-easterlies have kept the entire season freeze-dried and there are almost no swallows through the blue overhead, while the pipits, parachuting down in song display, whose notes are flat at the best of times, were picked to desultory shreds by the currents of cold air.

It was so dry that at least I could lie among the bilberry bushes to escape the wind and, there, in a condition of enforced sloth, I chanced upon a search method for the creature I'd come to see. On earlier visits I'd had tantalising bumblebee sightings in the middle distance over the moors, their course wandering and wind-blown, my eye tormented by the zigzag line, yet unmistakably bees that looked orange-bodied and deeply unfamiliar, and which seemed to vanish completely like a lizard's tail whipping down a hole.

Down here, however, under the bilberry canopy I gradually began to hear bees all around, trundling among the vegetation. With patience, and by parting the foliage like some giant in a forest, I found them crawling from one bilberry flower to another, tapping each pink bell for nectar, then barrelling through to the next.

They were mountain bumblebees, *Bombus monticola*, patchily distributed and declining and usually above 1,000 metres, and, arguably, the most beautiful of their British family. Their shoulders are dandelion yellow but much of the abdomen is a soft-apricot plush. They look like animate furry fruit bonbons. The queens hatch late and their preferred food is bilberry (another name is 'bilberry bumblebee') and heather, but here I could appreciate another of their adaptations to such a wind-battered environment. They weren't so much bumbling through the air like most of this insect group, but scrambling among a moss-softened understorey and, thus, keeping to a microclimate far warmer than the one just a few inches above.

## 17 May 2016

### ✍ CLAXTON, NORFOLK ✍

I can tell the weather by the St Mark's flies, because as they sail over the brambles, their forelegs dangle together and are held so that they face directly into the oncoming breeze and fractionally ahead of the body. Rather like a boat's keel, those legs keep the fly true in its relation to the airstream and they now point south-west.

Those warm winds brought the summer migrants streaming home. As I walk down the beck the whitethroats sing at intervals. They are lithe creatures adept at threading mouse-like through spiked vegetation. Two tiny extravagances of plumage are the ginger patches mainly in two wing feathers and a white powder puff at the throat, which swells up when they sing. Their repeated phrase is just two seconds long and is squirted out at a rate of thirteen a minute. Words fail before its complexity but old Scottish country names – 'churr muffit' and 'white lintie' – capture something of both the rubbery chatter and the momentary linnet's sweetness present in its coarser fabric.

The song is a perfect analogue of its bramble habitat: a mixture of thorny harshness but flushed here and there with the fresh green of blackberry leaves. It is even as lowly and modest as the bush from which it emerges. My guess is that many people who live and walk all summer long down whitethroat lanes never register the sound consciously. It inhabits our spring subliminally. It comes to us only in our dreams.

So would we notice if it never came at all? In 1969 ornithologists were so alarmed by the bird's no-show that they wrote a paper entitled simply: 'Where have all the whitethroats gone?' It was estimated that eight million of them had vanished. It turned out that whitethroats were as attached to acacia thorn as they are to bramble. When the African rains failed in the Sahel in the late 1960s, the birds were as badly affected as the region's fifty million people, many of whom were displaced or died because of drought. Whitethroats may creep among nettles but, as much as ourselves or the weather, they illuminate the interconnectedness of all life.

## 19 May 2015

### ⋙ TAN-Y-BWLCH, GWYNEDD ⋘

What a world it must have been! In their book on Britain's prehistoric bird populations the late Derek Yalden and Umberto Albarella speculated that our island's first forest blanket after the end of the last ice age held sixteen million wood warblers every spring. Now there are fewer than 35,000 and in the fifteen years since 1995 they declined nationally by 65 per cent.

These woods are one of their last strongholds and it emphasises how the creature's world is always in green: either the emerald of rainforest where they spend our winter or, as it is here, the astonishing chromatic patchwork of lichen, fern, moss, holly and fresh-licked leaves of beech and oak. The steep-sided place was so immersed in green that at times it felt as if we were under water. The warbler sealed the impression because as it sang it flew in short slow-wafted flurries from tree to tree. In each momentary shift the wings were rowing so deeply through tidal pools of sunlight that they looked like fins and the displaying birds like fish.

If the visual impact was aquatic then the music was stone. Wood warblers grind and quarry out their notes from some mysterious Pleistocene hoard and – with head back and wings quivering – spray them as flakes of sound in an ecstatic downward trill. The tempo builds steadily. At first the lapidary notes are granular and individual, then they blur to the human ear and as they accelerate they ignite like a match-lit burst of light in that green place.

This song seems like light and in truth it is made from light. Think this: the light in the red spectrum is swallowed by all the chloroplasts that make Tan-y-Bwlch so green, then the leaf becomes moth larva and the caterpillar turns to muscle and surplus energy in a bird. Wood warbler and wood and song are all just light. We too come from light. In this spot and at that moment we all felt it. How strange to think that this tiny bird comes out of Africa to make these woods so completely Welsh. What a world we still own now!

## 20 May 2014

### ↣ CLAXTON, NORFOLK ↢

It set out almost exactly to the day seventy-seven years ago and must have presented a very strange vision. It was a removal column heading from north Devon for Stiffkey on the Norfolk coast. It mixed elements of aristocratic high style with travellers' poverty and moved at a painfully slow pace, averaging at times just eight miles an hour. For the full 300 miles to its destination it took two and a half days.

First came an old-style caravan towed by an open-topped Alvis Silver Eagle, one of those impressive early cars with long bonnets and enormous front-wheel arches shaped rather like diving otters. Next came a dilapidated lorry, broken down and gasping, followed by its long trailer topped by a dinghy.

The picturesque column marked the beginning of a ten-year spell in East Anglia by the large family of the author Henry

Williamson. Behind lay a long residence in the Devonshire countryside, while ahead lay their experimental foray into Norfolk farming. In some ways the decade spent in East Anglia marked a transition in Williamson's literary reputation. His first Devonshire period had involved substantial celebrity and success, especially after the publication of his award-winning classic, *Tarka the Otter*.

To come were years of backbreaking hard labour, entanglement in right-wing politics, controversy, even arrest, vilification and eventual divorce. Yet the time at Stiffkey would also bear fruit in two notable books centred on the Norfolk landscape, Williamson's strange, fitfully beautiful study of a rare gamebird, *The Phasian Bird* (1948), but also a minor classic entitled *The Story of a Norfolk Farm* (1941). His completion of the latter work just before World War Two in 1939 has its seventy-fifth anniversary this year.

It describes how Williamson, who was the most celebrated nature writer of his day, had become disillusioned after almost two decades of near-constant literary production. Instinctively this lover of wildlife and landscape sought spiritual refreshment through a more intimate engagement with the soil. Hence his fateful decision to buy a 200-acre farm complete with several cottages on the north Norfolk coast for just over £2,000.

He had no experience of farming and when he bought the place British agriculture was just at the end of its long depression. Yet Williamson rose to his Sisyphean challenge with extraordinary stamina. The book is an account of his life as a builder or repairer of cottages, stockyards, stables and roads. It narrates his perpetual conflict with rats, thistles, rabbits, debt, defective machinery and what he saw as the straitjacketed mindset and hidebound traditions of his Norfolk farmhands.

In fairness Williamson never fudges his own shortcomings, nor does he stint in praise for his hardworking foreman and the other staff. Between them they turned a derelict wasteland of weeds and infertility into a grade-one farm. Yet Williamson also had an agenda beyond mere agriculture.

He saw his own mid-life crisis, which coincided with the interwar period of English history, as reflective of a wider malaise in the nation's affairs. His search for self-renewal was assumed to mirror Britain's own need for spiritual refreshment. The problem, in short, was money. The country had mortgaged its soul to business and profit. Its bowels were beset by what Williamson memorably called the 'golden tapeworm'. The remedy, he thought, lay in proper relations to land. No nation could flourish as long as it neglected its soil.

Behind these ideas were Williamson's wider assertion that the spirit of humankind was fulfilled when the individual aligned him- or herself with the wider flux of existence, that stream of ancient sunlight which had nourished the Earth since time immemorial and was the very source of life itself. These were enormously rich and fine sentiments.

Sadly when it came to finding political outlet for these ideas Williamson saw hope in the new rise of the far right abroad and of Oswald Mosley's British Union of Fascists at home. It was this alignment that has, to some extent, blighted Williamson's later reputation and for many in his underground following, obscured his literary achievement, which was especially expressed through an astonishing fifteen-novel sequence entitled *A Chronicle of Ancient Sunlight*.

What is beyond dispute is that Williamson wrote books about animal life – *Tarka the Otter*, *Salar the Salmon*, etc. – that have few equals in this country. His gift for intuiting and expressing the effects of wild places and creatures upon the human imagination is also writ large in *The Story of a Norfolk Farm*.

Of Stiffkey in summer, he wrote, 'We sat down on the grass, gazing out over the marshes, one vast gut-channered prairie of pale blue sea-lavender. Afar was the sea merging in summer mist and the palest azure sky. There was no sound: the air was still: not a bird was stirring. This was the sun I remembered from boyhood days, the ancient harvest sunshine of that perished time when the earth was fresh and summer seemed an illimitable shining that would never end, the reapers moving round the fields and setting up the stooks of golden corn. And sitting there, it was as though the past and present were one again.'

Equally indisputable was Williamson's stomach for hard work. In his account of the Stiffkey years he describes how he shifted 1,000 tons of hard material on to the farm's internal roads, spread 100 tons of dyke silt on to the arable land, cut 40 tons of firewood from 1,000 yards of hedge and spread 300 tons of chalk on to his fields. While he had supervised all that labour, this novelist of English life had also written 400,000 words of new books. That is a writer and a man one cannot dismiss without fair hearing.

# JUNE

2 June 2015

Recently my search for the eggs laid by orange-tip butterflies on my fen has become a brief obsession. Finding something smaller than a fly's eye is nowhere near as impressive – or immodest – as it may sound. Once you have the search image pre-loaded in your head it's just a case of lifting the flowerheads one at a time until you locate the telltale grooved flask glued to the stalk.

Since orange-tips use just two plant species, I search either the garlic-mustard or, preferably in this wet site, the pale-pink blooms of lady's smock. What makes the task easiest of all is that the eggs, while only 1–2 millimetres long, are fluorescent orange. Presumably they are so bright, not to facilitate my game, but to alert predators that here is something unpleasant to eat.

The adult male insect has wings of the same intense colour and I learnt recently in Peter Marren's forthcoming book, *Rainbow Dust* (Square Peg), which is the distilled essence from an entire lifetime's reading, looking and taking pleasure in butterflies, that those orange orbs warn of acrid mustard oils accumulated in the creature's body.

What gives me real satisfaction in finding butterfly eggs is partly pride that such a beautiful creature should choose my ground to propagate its kind. Deeper still is the fulfilment that comes from appreciating how little of life is accessible to our own gross perception. An egg the size of a pin-head is a humbling indicator of an entire dimension we normally miss.

There is an ancillary delight in knowing how that orange capsule, if it hatches successfully, will morph into a caterpillar resembling the lady's smock's seed pod. For eight further months it will then rest as a brown chrysalis disguised as a thorn. Then next May it will emerge as one of the most heart-gladdening creatures in a heart-gladdening month. But what makes that grain of life most affecting of all is that it belongs to my neighbour at Blackwater who navigates and orders their experience through chemical vapours called pheromones that I will never see nor know. Yet I can intuit that complex other world in something as simple and true as an orange egg.

## 5 June 2018

### ⤙ GARRON POINT, ABERDEENSHIRE ⤚

Beyond Sandend village and the slow white waves running into its sunlit bay, there was this wilderness of guano-nourished grass and three northward-facing ribs of metamorphosed sedimentary rock. The latter were tilted on end and weathered along their joints so that the gulls on the raised slabs of ancient stone were spaced in heraldic assembly.

Through the luxuriant hummocks by the cliff edge I manoeuvred with an old man's caution, which was more than just fear of falling. The wailing of the birds created a wrap-around atmosphere of such density and chaos that I was almost unbalanced by it.

There were perhaps 1,000 pairs of herring gulls. It is the same species that knocks ice cream from toddlers' hands, the one that journalists delight to report upon drawing blood from Yorkshire terriers or old ladies' heads. Yet British herring gulls have declined from 286,000 pairs in 1970 to just 132,000 by 2002. These figures reveal a further scandal because, for sixteen years, successive governments have failed to update this survey of our seabird populations, for which this country is more important than almost any other in Europe. Of herring gulls, for example, we hold an eighth of the world's total.

Here at Garron Point you can see the birds purged of all human association. I loved the way that, as each gull yowled its part in the birds' unceasing shanty, its head half-turned like a clockwork toy. Then one would suddenly unleash a drawn-out territorial note known technically as the 'long-call'. The bird would brace itself, legs planted wide, to withstand the impact of its own internal eruption. The head would point down, then up, and, with bill wide open, it would vomit up this huge sea sound that gains in volume as the gorge and head rise heavenwards.

Above the calling birds, others sailed in to land. Down the gull would come on upraised span, the evening sun visible through the frayed tail edges, the southerlies lifting slight ruffles of coverts among the silvered wings and the bird, holding the opposing powers of wind and gravity in momentary balance, would descend in a blaze of reflected light with the long lyrate curves of an angel.

6 June 2017

CLAXTON, NORFOLK

Almost as if they were flowers that had bulbed up out of the ground overnight, house martins were suddenly all about our house. Every year the pairs in the village perform an almost ritualised house inspection, when they check all the neighbouring properties for suitable nest sites. And every time they tantalise me by swooping to examine even our non-existent eaves.

They then fuss about the gable end to our neighbour's bungalow. Were they ever to choose this last spot, which looks perfect to my unbirdlike eyes, it would bring their distillate of African sunshine to within metres of my office. For a day or two the trench of green space between our houses is threaded with the dazzle of their weighted blue lines. Down and under, back and away.

I will them to make that pattern of flight their summer practice and, thus, part of the fabric of my work day. But no. More troubling than this private disappointment is a decline in our village house martins, which reflects how half of the British population has been lost since 1970.

It was wonderful, therefore, to see them in Greece a week later where the numbers seem undiminished. There was one rain-fed moment when a puddle by the village of Psarades, on the edge of Lake Prespa, was a martin magnet. How strange that this blunt-bodied blue bird, which seems so much a creature of pure air, has this brief intimacy with bare earth.

Time and again fifty martins plumped down on to one tiny patch of wet track. Their feet got so glued to it that the wings were fluttering as if to keep them free, while they bent and stubbed tiny mouths on to the mud. There were glistening droplets of it all over their backs and breasts and off they would fly with untidy hods of building stuff packed on to their beaks. It was an extraordinary blend of grey earth and singing lazuline air.

It occurred to me, as they trafficked their annual construction materials, which they must have carried above our heads for more than a million of our shared cave-dwelling years, that maybe martins taught humans how to build houses.

## 7 June 2016

### CLAXTON, NORFOLK

There had to be some benefits to the year's strange grey iron-clad winter–spring, which persisted right until last month in our area. Now we see them in the late coming of our may blossom. The hedges have turned into great waves of flowering luxuriance and, although the showing was strong in 2013 after its own cold-blasted start, I cannot recall a better hawthorn display.

One wonderful feature is the branches so loaded with blossom that they dangle about the bushes in great tentacles of sweetness. One feels even more enfolded in spring's plenty. Another intriguing detail is the degree of stronger pink colour in the more typical white tide. The gene creating this effect is presumably the one that was isolated by growers and eventually gave us that coral-flowered hawthorn cultivar that is so beloved of town councils. I have wild bushes near me where a whole outer third of the white petals are infused with rose and en masse they give it a gloriously subtle hue, like a bowl's last residue of strawberry juice amid the double cream.

A secondary pleasure from hawthorn is the wonderfully ambiguous perfume which, at its best, in the tunnel-like hedges down our lane, is an entire sensory atmosphere. If it smells of flesh, as some people propose, then it is the most innocent of all, reminding me of that wonderful fragrance of newborn babies.

What makes such a landscape-sized display so much more satisfying than any garden flower show are the incidental details that create an entire seasonal moment: the fly-hum veil around the hedges, the morning's late dew upon your boots, the granular alarm notes of wrens disturbed at their own hawthorn business, ragged outlines of moulting rooks overhead, sedge warblers mimicking linnets and Hereford cattle clanging the metal gate as they scratch away all that fly itch. Most telling of all, however, is the double act the hawthorns perform with cow parsley so that on many approach roads to Claxton they create the brief white-walled lanes of high spring. They lend to these Saxon latitudes a momentary sense of upwelling tropicality.

## 9 June 2014

### ⤙ HIGHBURY WOODS, GLOUCESTERSHIRE ⤚

Rain cloud loomed and passed, loomed and passed in successive dark waves all day, but the drizzle was without end. By the time we had flogged up the steep hill from the village of Redbrook, our wet-weather gear was soaked within and without. Yet it was worth it. Somewhere beyond that wall of vegetation were sixty-five million other Britons, but all we had of them was the faint drum of traffic on the A466.

We entered a world an East Anglian never knows: a place of fern and tree that love the wetter conditions of the west. Large-leaved lime, broad buckler fern, spleenwort, hart's-tongue and polypody – even the names sound exotic. No patch of tropical rainforest could have been wetter or greener. A long line of ancient dark yews and beech trees, which ran all across this steep ridge high above the River Wye, sealed us under the closed canopy and we were cocooned in warm damp emerald air. In some places there were holloways so tunnel-like it felt as if we were journeying into the Earth, not passing over it.

In fact it was so steeped in deep green at times it looked almost black; until we saw a blackbird dash through the tangle and we got our true chromatic bearings once more. Yet the verb 'to see' really overstates the nature of these avian encounters: they were just fragmented, Cubist glimpses of glossy black wing or orange beak. There was nothing broken about the song, however. It was as constant as the rain. At times in those Wye Valley woods, when you can stand in some open field, with the dense trees cloaked on all horizons, the oily brown Wye itself muscling downstream, it was as if blackbird music, rich and soft-soiled, rose like steam from them all. The bird's very blackness seemed the essence of all that chlorophyll and the song itself a higher distillate of everything green and free. It is England reduced to sound and no tourist-drawing, ruined, famous abbey could express it more truly.


10 June 2013

◈ CLAXTON, NORFOLK ◈

I remember a Derbyshire wag once quipping that 'May' seldom comes before June in the Peak District. His joke hinged on an alternative name for hawthorn, the May tree. Little did I ever imagine that his pun would have meaning in Norfolk. Yet this year that totemic show of luminous blossom which, in recent years, has begun here as early as April, has been shifted back a whole month by the coldest winter.

My goodness, however, has it been worth the wait! It's one of the best displays I can recall. There's one bush on the marsh that is so smothered in flowers I feel I have to go back constantly to enjoy it one last time. Most normal flowering hawthorns involve a quintessential salad freshness that flows from the combination of milky blossoms and green foliage. In this bush, however, the leaves are almost completely enfolded in the gently domed sprays of petals. It looks less like May than December – as if the whole shrub has been enveloped in a great deluge of snow.

In truth hawthorn is never virgin white like snow. Every rosette has about twenty stamens – that are tipped a glorious pale plum in peak condition – and these accumulate on the whole bush as tens of thousands of tiny points of darkness in the galaxy of cream. Hawthorn is ever so minutely sullied and rendered exquisitely impure by the processes of reproduction, which makes it such a perfect metaphor for spring.

That ambiguous note is mirrored nicely by the odour, which the writer Geoffrey Grigson thought best enjoyed in small doses. In his own cornucopia of plant lore, *Flora Britannica*, Richard Mabey suggested that hawthorn actually smells of sex. Yet I cannot detect that precise perfume. To me, it has a deep undertow of sweetness like honey, or like flowering meadowsweet, but through it, mingling with it, is something darker, something off-key, perhaps, like faint raw rubber; not malign, but definitely not innocent.


16 June 2015

CLAXTON, NORFOLK

I knew they lived in the parish but I'd only seen them from a distance six years ago. There'd been no formal introduction, as it were, but today we met properly for the first time; on the lane down to the marsh where the dog walkers go. The surroundings were modest for June: a green light so dark and immersive it felt like liquid. On one side were the silver heads of false oat grass. On the other was a shelf of fresh bramble backed by a wall of hawthorn and over and through all that green shadow a blackbird soloed to the morning.

The yellow-barred longhorn has to be one of the weirdest moths in England. It is a common and widespread insect but, judging from my own experience, easily overlooked or mistaken for something mundane. When they were flying over the hawthorn tops they were no more than dark flies, dancing and skittering in motion but otherwise lacking any kind of attention-requiring detail.

Then they would descend, glancing around me in a restless random pattern reminiscent of a gnat swarm. There were about a dozen. All males. They gravitated to a sliver of sunlight through the trees and were essentially pale glinting brown. What was most impressive were the long threads of what looked like limbs wafting as they moved. But those so-called 'longhorns' are actually antennae four times longer than their owner's body. The tension generated by flight bent the glistening threads to either side and above their passage so that it looked as if they were bobbing up and down on a child's swing of their own making.

Occasionally a yellow-barred longhorn would land. Then, the featureless insect above the hawthorn or the brown glancing fly looping in its home-made swing became a flake of gold attached to two wind-brushed blond hairs. Almost at every step in this season something remarkable makes our acquaintance. Perhaps it is because as I get older I walk more slowly and have more encounters of this kind. Maybe it is also the years that make such moments more moving and important.

## 20 June 2017

#### ≫ AIGAS FIELD CENTRE, HIGHLANDS ≪

Just ten minutes down the valley from this outstanding educational institute is the largest goat willow in Britain. The veteran is tucked away at the roadside amid a line of alders and so sunk in a deep and almost subaquatic gloom that you could easily miss it. A visit also requires a minor girding of loins to brave the midge-laden atmosphere, although meeting the tree on intimate terms is worth any amount of insect nuisance.

As if one spectacular specimen were not enough, the willow has stood by the side of the same wild cherry for possibly two centuries. The latter is also among the ten largest of its kind recorded in Britain and, like its neighbour, is an entire ecosystem unto itself. Many of the branches are tusks of smooth ivory-white timber that have been riddled by woodpeckers or beetles, while the main boll is an elephant's belly of heartwood smothered in mosses, lichens and ferns.

The cherry is wonderful but it is modest in comparison with the structure of its companion. The willow was a sapling when the Battle of Culloden was fought and some combatants must have passed it on their way to war. The tree seems to have secured its own survival by throwing out successive trunks, each of which has eventually collapsed under its own weight and succumbed to rot. Then at the places where these limbs have all fallen they have re-rooted and risen again as more fresh uprights.

No single photograph can do justice to all these avatars. In fact, even tracing the genetic connections between one part and the next is difficult, because the fallen trunks have sometimes rotted away completely and their replacement limbs look like several separate trees. Yet via this mechanism of death and resurrection one vegetative organism has managed to step over 2 metres of water-filled dyke and spread outwards across more than 15 metres of ground. Despite a livid-green pelage of moss, the whole thing has an oddly spider-like quality for me. I am struck also by the way the willow expresses the richness entailed in a long-drawn-out death, as much as the merits of one magnificently enduring life.


## 21 June 2016

### ⤐ Aigas Field Centre, Highlands ⤏

For all their recent spread and increase, until they now skirt the edges of several Scottish cities and pop up occasionally even in England as far south as Shropshire, pine martens are still rare and hard to see. This field study centre, with its dedicated hides and long-established feeding programme, must be one of the best places in the country to watch them. The closest I'd come in the previous forty years were glimpses of a close relative, the beech marten, dead at the sides of Greek roads.

So when one came bounding through the shadow towards us, it was a wonderful moment. The first powerful impressions were of its noiseless movements and shape. It undulated through the trees in such soft eel-like loops that one could imagine it was an animal lacking in bone and composed merely of muscle and cartilage. There was one extraordinary moment when it scaled a tree stump to take food from the top. As it rose upwards the body and tail were pulled taut so that it resembled a furry snake. Then all that liquid flesh was drawn up as if by peristalsis, when the creature wound about the post crown, balancing on nothing more than 2x2 in python coils of air-filled fur.

The full range of colours was complex. The long guard hairs on the back, haunches and rear flanks glistened as if they had been sprayed with hair lacquer. The hind neck, head and forelegs had the sort of fur shade you see in photographs of society women of a certain vintage, when sable coats were assumed to be expressions of luxurious style, and not needless cruelty. Then there was the bib down the chin and upper breast – a mixture of citrus and pale apricot that somehow captured all of your attention throughout its antics.

Oblivious of its audience and the camera shutters, it scampered over logs, heaved at stones to uncover food stores, chomped on nuts with open relish, tricked along poles to slurp up honey and faded gradually into the gloom, under pine, until all that was clearly visible were the lemon outlines to two black ears dancing over quick silence.

## 23 June 2014

### CLAXTON, NORFOLK

At this range the dead vole is little more than a slumped arc of cooling fur clamped in the cage of a barn owl's dangling feet. Centred perfectly beneath those outspread wings, it seems now like the dark pivot to animate the smooth engine stroke of the bird's vanishing flight. Aside from this minute drama the morning calm is conspicuous. There are the quiet ramble of reed warblers and the fussing cluck of moorhens somewhere in a dyke but, otherwise, I am immersed in the full-blossomed quietude of mid-June.

Then I see it and realise I must have passed without registering for several days in succession another scene of microscopic turmoil. It is a larval colony of peacock butterflies. The nettle stand is crazed around by a tangle of cleavers, while above it, standing proud of the canopy like miniature flat-topped acacias, are the white umbels of hogweed. These other plants are completely untouched but the nettles have been ravaged by the jaws of scores of black caterpillars. Many leaves and stems are silvered with a kind of glistening slime left by the insects or the foliage is enmeshed in larval silk. Where the insects have fed concertedly, I could still make out the nettle leaves' original spread, but only by the old networks of uneaten, dried veins that now seem as fragile as spiders' webs.

The caterpillars, by contrast, are luxuriant creatures: fat tubes of black velvet freckled with intense white spots. Adding a macabre touch to their appearance are sharp bristles that encircle the caterpillar's whole girth. Their owners emphasise the protective function of this armoury by lashing their upper bodies back and forth. Unfortunately neither nettle venom nor pointed spikes are complete defence against the ichneumon wasp, with its predatory blend of black and orange, that lurks in this same nettle patch. The insect will attempt to lay its eggs in or on the bodies of the peacock caterpillars after which the ichneumon larva will eat its host alive.

## 24 June 2013

### ⤳ CLAXTON, NORFOLK ⤺

Our dog-rose hedge, which skirts the road past the house, follows the local pattern for blossom this summer, with the most abundant flowering I can recall. There are about 100 brilliant magenta blooms but several hundred more buds, all cued to open in the coming days, are clasped in their five sepals like a closed hand over a tiny scroll of pink paper.

The whole hedge is bumblebee heaven. Initially I was slightly puzzled why all belonged to just one species. There are seven common garden bumblebees, but the dog roses seemed the exclusive preserve of a beauty called the tree bumblebee. It's among the easiest to identify because it combines a unique colour combination of broad white tip to the dark abdomen (its 'bum', if you will), with a bright fox-brown thorax.

Remarkably this insect has only been in the country for about twelve years and there is still a faintly exotic, presumably Gallic, tone to the tree bumblebee's buzz. For the first ever was discovered in 2001 near Southampton by Dave Goulson, creator of the Bumblebee Conservation Trust and author of a recent wonderful book, *A Sting in the Tale*. Over just twelve generations tree bumblebees have swept the country. I first spotted one here three years ago amid a state of high excitement and confusion – what on Earth could it be? – but since then I cannot seem to help seeing them almost everywhere. Today the species has reached as far north as Iceland.

I eventually worked out why our hedge was so much the territory of this insect when I finally traced the flight path to their nest, which was literally seconds away from all that dog-rose nectar and pollen. True to the name these bumblebees nest above ground often in tree cavities, but this particular colony has found a ready substitute under one of the pantiles on our roof. The nest, in fact, seems to lie exactly above the spot where I'm writing these words.

### 25 June 2012

#### ⟾ CLAXTON, NORFOLK ⟾

Just three repeated notes rang out with the volume of an alarm clock so that I was minded to check the time. It was 3.35 a.m. They were the first bars of a song thrush's morning song. High and shrill, they came through the curtains like silver shards in the smoky pre-dawn dullness.

I sense that song thrush song evolves over the spring and it achieves its finest quality about now. The birds are so widespread, from Claxton to Kinlochbervie, from Kennijack to Kirkwall, that everyone could hear one. I recommend you take out the earphones or pull back the plate glass and yield to the song of song thrushes. The sound will cease in a few weeks' time. But when it first begins in those far-off, leafless, ungreen landscapes of February and March the bird's clean hard notes come pounding over the fields like cannonfire. The full dark canopies of June, however, soften and somehow enrich the sound and I love it most in the evenings when the thrush himself, now well practised but perhaps busy with nests and chicks, seems less committed and mellower. The song lines sail out over the village, enfolding us all like the joy notes from distant church bells.

Its main competitors for our premier bird music are the wonderful, insinuating, complex melodies of the blackbird. But blackbirds are not just ours. You can hear them just as well on Turkey's Lycian shore, or in the Elburz Mountains of Iran, and westwards as far as those dark oleander-filled valleys of Andalusia. In fact you could carry on to the pre-desert, to those fig-shaded oadis of the Anti-Atlas and still find Morocco's dawn filled with blackbird. But song thrush song is altogether more restricted. The music has about it the smell of damp oakwoods and the scent of pine, to which habitats the song of the song thrush brings an invincible sense of hope. One wonders if it was for these reasons that last time the British voted it their favourite birdsong?

25 June 2014

CLAXTON, NORFOLK

I wonder how many people share my passion for brambles? Instead of treating them as hook-clawed monsters that need culling, in our garden we are highly tolerant of the bushes. We now have a 20-foot bramble hedge that by midsummer is smothered in those glorious soft pink blooms.

My cultivation of this often unloved plant is not just self-interest. I cherish them because my neighbours love bramble blossom too. I'm thinking especially of bumblebees. Find a particularly floriferous patch and you will soon recognise that these glorious insects and brambles go together just as much as apples and blackberries. I know small patches locally that attract twelve species of bumblebee, which is half the British complement.

There are about 240 species worldwide and real bumblebee heaven is in the mountains of Asia, especially the high-altitude regions of eastern Tibet. It is likely that bumblebees originated somewhere near there and spread westwards into Europe, sixteen million years before the earliest hominids had even evolved. It is worth reflecting, when you next see one of these insects that, despite its fizzing aura of speed and busyness, you are witness to an immensely venerable lineage. Bumblebees probably pre-date our own species by thirty-five million years.

Part of the joy of the insects, however, is undoubtedly that immense sense of now. Follow any single individual worker and she will visit scores of flowerheads in any minute, very often dismissing those that have already been drained of nectar and looking for the next bloom rich in supplies of sweetness or pollen. Once the honey-stomach is full of liquid sugar – a cargo that can weigh almost as much as the bee itself – and the pollen baskets on its hind legs are so large it looks like an escaped convict's ball-and-chain, the creature rises into the air to head back to the nest chamber. It is hardly surprising that the average worker lives little more than two to six weeks.

There is another measure of the extraordinarily rapid lifestyles of bumblebees. One of the commonest British species is called tree bumblebee. It is easy to recognise because of a unique colour combination involving a warm brown thorax and a prominent white tip to the abdomen. Tree bumblebees are almost certainly in your garden this morning, but have only just colonised much of Britain in the last thirteen years.

Despite this positive development, we cannot feel equally pleased about the tree bumblebee's relatives. All the British species have declined, some catastrophically, and only seven are now considered common. Ironically, two of the acute challenges come from the bumblebees' relative, the honeybee. Commercial hives are now so commonplace that these domesticated insects are undoubtedly competitors for the supplies of pollen and nectar required by wild bees.

Worse in many ways, and an issue that has me grinding my teeth in frustration whenever I hear it repeated, is our fixation with the plight of honeybees. Don't misunderstand me: honeybees are wonderful and so too are their ambrosial products. As many of us now know, they face major threats themselves from introduced problems, such as varroa mites, and from the side-effects of pesticides called neonicotinoids. So deleterious are these chemicals that the EU has introduced a two-year ban, despite our own government's reluctance to accept the extensive proof of their impact.

However, it is depressing that honeybees get almost all the attention and are usually the only insects blessed for the incredibly important gift of pollination. In truth, those services, whose profits to us far exceed $100 billion worldwide, are performed by hundreds if not thousands of insect species in Britain alone. There are, for example, more than 250 bee species in this country, while pollination is also undertaken by a suite of others like beetles and moths. Truly we should cherish and thank them all.

Bumblebees are such important pollinators that it is likely the tomatoes in your salad throughout this summer will be owed partly to them. Something like a million commercially reared bumblebee colonies are sold and exported worldwide for use in industrial vegetable and fruit production. To acknowledge the immense economic importance of bumblebees would at least be a start in challenging the myth of the honeybee's supposedly solitary role.

Aside from pesticides and competition, bumblebees face another challenge from a reduction in their habitats. There has been a nationwide decline in wild flowers in our countryside, but also in our towns and gardens. So often now people prefer lawns free of everything but short turf or, worse still, replace it altogether with tarmac, decking and bark chippings.

In our civic space we seem to be obsessed with tidiness, as if the natural world around our homes should be an extension of our house interiors – free of any growth or disorder. Yet bumblebees thrive on neglect – in those corners of fields, on

grass verges or roundabouts and in gardens where people omit
to deploy the lawnmower and strimmer. So this summer I
recommend you do yourself a favour: put away the mower, let
the wild flowers flourish and perhaps string up your hammock.
From that horizontal position you should delight to watch the
busyness of bees. Rest assured: your leisure is their profit.

There are two wonderful organisations campaigning exclusively
for insects in this country: Buglife is the nation's main
invertebrate champion and membership organisation. Details at
http://www.buglife.org.uk or Buglife, Age UK, The Lindens,
86 Lincoln Road, Peterborough PEI 2SN. Details about
the Bumblebee Conservation Trust can be found at www.
bumblebeeconservation.org.

## 30 June 2015

### ⤞ CLAXTON, NORFOLK ⤝

Through the hedge on the path to the marsh I could hear
their commotion. Eight sharp-tipped hoofs stabbing the
ground and then, at last, a telltale blur of orange flanks
that revealed them as Chinese water deer. Males squared up
in combat. As my binoculars dialled into crisp detail they
instantly answered a long-standing mystery. For years I've
found handfuls of loose deer hair strewn on the ground, but
was always puzzled why it was shed in that fashion. Here was
the answer.

The male deer possess long canines in the upper jaw that
slot either side of the closed mouth like fangs. Each buck, facing
his opponent, now feinted and jinked for the opening to land
its charge, until one would finally dash at the other. The rushes
were ferocious. The assailant often performed full somersaults
over its rival, rolling back upon back, legs flailing down in an
instant search for new purchase. And once it landed the deer

would curve around the head of its enemy, gouging sharp teeth into the other's flank. Fur flew.

One finally yielded but not before they had rested in unison, slack mouths wide open, hard-breathed, red-gummed and the teeth of these teddy-bear deer of such sweet mien momentarily suggested nothing less than something sabre-toothed and predatory.

It had all unfolded to the iambic heart-pounded rhythm of sex, but the next day at Blackwater I encountered a reproductive drama whose denouement was but 2 centimetres across, yet it contained a poetry that was darker, harder, more fertile. We were looking for spiders until one of us came upon a dead dung fly with its legs hugged entirely round a blade of grass. The whole posture was bizarre. The abdomen curved back and up, but the head was forward and down as if a fly were bowing in abject submission. Its whole body glistened with something like sugar frosting, but these were the spores of mould called *Entomophthora*. Over seven days it consumes the fly within and then by some biochemical trick, fashioned through the millennia, it persuades the fly brain that its owner should die in an attitude suited to the dispersal of its own spores.

# JULY

~☙ CLAXTON, NORFOLK ☙~

If I set aside the rag-winged rooks and moulting lapwings and forget the storms that this land has just endured, the morning seems utterly still. I stand to watch a long flotilla of cumulus over the marsh as beautiful and unmoving as sail ships becalmed in doldrums. There is so little breeze that neither foreground nettle nor the red-tinged Yorkshire fog beyond so much as stirs.

Even with my coarse senses, however, I know that this rain-washed stillness is volatile and densely scented. There is a deer nudging through the reeds that I shall never see because it navigates by smell. There is a foul blast of musk that its owner left last night on the path and it is now so clogged with stink you would think that Claxton had no other chemistry but that of fox.

There are moths here that can follow pheromone trails to potential mates across 8 kilometres of intervening ground. And bumblebees of four species, threading the dog rose in our garden, add to the flowers their own micro-trace of scent from their feet and bodies that inform other bees exactly which blooms have been visited and drained.

Finally there is a dead vole. Who knows what necrotic vapour winds through the square of light above where it lies on the path, but black ants are already prospecting its corpse. More than any other, these insects allow us to reflect upon a chemical realm we can seldom know empirically.

Ants, which have a total biomass equal to that of all humanity, are governed by it. They lay pheromone trails that their sisters can follow and the man who first researched these invisible tramlines, E. O. Wilson, proposed that a single microgram of pheromone, if laid with maximum efficiency, would be enough to send billions of ants three times round our planet.

The space I look across and view as clear air is in truth a cataract of molecules guiding life in all its trades. Yet that entire grand bazaar of old summer chemistry is all blended to me now and I can pick out just one clear note: the first crisp whiff of autumn.

## 7 July 2014

### ⌒ BLACKWATER CARR, NORFOLK ⌒

For several years now in my wooded fen I've been favouring a bramble patch by clipping out all competitors and creating space for the outlying shoots. It has slowly expanded but this spring it has grown with fresh confidence, sending out curving red-taloned arms 2.5 metres into the sky. It is fascinating to see how, after a period of strong winds, the patch has become a casualty of its own formidable armoury. Scores of new leaves are covered in self-inflicted tears where they have been battered against the spines on other parts of the bush.

Yet July brambles mingle a pale-pink generosity with all this aggression. The flower season may be past its best and from the middle of each withered old bloom emerges the knobbly green tonsure of a fresh berry, complete with its hairline of dead stamens, but there is sweetness still in my bramble to satisfy a million insects. In an hour's search I found so many flies I couldn't name I finally understood how, after forty years of observation, I knew next to nothing about British nature.

There was consolation in the dazzle of commas or red admirals and in the commuter traffic of vestal cuckoo, garden and common carder bumblebees. Even just the warmth of the leaves seemed a lure for the wonderfully named marmalade hoverflies and a stoop-backed relative with bug eyes called *Volucella bombylans*. Then my bramble patch repaid my loving care with a rarer gift. The red-tipped clearwing is one of a strange and highly localised group of moths whose appearance mimics various species of stinging insects. I've seen clearwings on just five occasions ever and the hornet clearwing looks so like its namesake it is uncanny. Luxuriating in this perpetual traffic of life, and immersed in the songs of wrens or whitethroats and the bass gravel notes of crows, I began to see how this great breast of thorn with its pastel-toned orbit of flower and nectar is an entire world unto itself – intricate, evolving and beautiful.

## 7 July 2015

### ⌦ CLAXTON, NORFOLK ⌫

'The garden looks wonderfully crazy' were our daughter's first words when she came home last week. If it is as she says, then it's the most patiently acquired craziness you can imagine. It started nine years ago when I left one edge of our lawn unmown. In short order it acquired new residents among the hitherto rigidly controlled monoculture.

A patch of marjoram moved in and, in turn, provided accommodation for a gorgeous moth called the small purple and gold, not to mention a colony of field grasshoppers. Under the new laissez-faire regime, ragwort and sneezewort began to bloom. A breakthrough came five years ago with the appearance of spear thistle and hogweed. The latter's platforms of white-flowered sweetness attract about a dozen hoverfly species daily and a glittering host of pollen beetles. Another new neighbour, who possesses the gem-like beauty of polished malachite, is the swollen-thighed beetle.

Last autumn I gave the patch another nudge by sowing corncockle and yellow rattle. The latter is particularly useful because it's a hemiparasite that further reduces the dominance of grass. It bore new riches this spring with an additional swathe of yellow blooms and its own musical orbit of a thousand bumblebees. They've now performed their pollinating duties and as the yellow rattle seed sets, so the ox-eye daisies and the fox-and-cubs are in their pomp. This month and last I've had a rotating cycle of thirteen pollen- and nectar-bearing plants.

I would be the first to admit that my patch lacks the true 'wildness' of a genuine flower meadow. In truth, sneezewort and fox-and-cubs are non-native introductions, while the corncockle and yellow rattle are here by formal invitation. The lawn edge is also so small as to seem insignificant. Yet it does have the genuinely unscripted vigour and adventure of a semi-natural habitat. And who knows what will arrive next? It also acquires some of its meaning from the fact that we've lost 99 per cent of our flower-rich meadows, yet there are at least one million acres of lawn in Britain. Maybe the real madness is that we haven't yet liberated all these potential spaces from the tyranny of the lawnmower.

8 July 2013

TARBERT, HARRIS

With all the unnecessary zeal of a reformed smoker I usually adopt a lofty moralising tone towards twitching, but especially towards my own disreputable rare-bird-chasing past. To think I once drove overnight from Scilly to Aberdeen to see an isabelline wheatear! Back then I was consumed by the thought that it was the third British record ever. Now I reflect on a different kind of consumption. Was all that carbon really well spent?

However, I recently discovered that there are ways to re-engage with the old twitching habit and still feel absolved from all its wickedness. It occurs on those very few occasions when it is you who finds the rare bird that all the others want to chase. We were in the port of Tarbert on the hunt for its famous tweed, when out of a Hebridean smoor swooped a bird from our dreams. A white-throated needletail is the ultimate paradox: a swift species with huge gravitas. It originates in China but thinks nothing of spending its winters in Australia. It is, in fact, the world's fastest bird in level flight and, unbelievable though it seemed to us, the eighth example ever to be seen in these islands was suddenly careering over our heads.

Instantly phone calls were made and within moments lives all over Britain were being re-oriented towards Harris. The most amusing moment came the following day. Watching one friend go from jibbering anxiety to exultant delirium (when he finally saw the bird) was like watching an addict eventually get his fix. Another friend I hadn't seen for twenty years suddenly sprang up in front of me. He had been in Leeds the previous afternoon. One carload had even driven from Kent to Inverness, then flown to Stornoway.

How sad that this extraordinary creature should end its days through collision with a nearby wind turbine. But it did at least achieve immortality of a sort. Next day it was front-page news in the Scottish edition of the *Sun*.

## 9 July 2012

### ❦ CLAXTON, NORFOLK ❦

I stand at dusk with an eyed hawkmoth perched at the tip of my left index finger. At this hour the light is so reduced that it looks nothing more than a bizarre, curve-bodied, weird-winged silhouette poised against the grey. Strange as it may seem, this moment is the end part of a weekly ritual that lasts for most of Sunday.

I catch the moths overnight in a trap and then at dawn switch it off and seal the lid. By Sunday morning proper, after breakfast, I unfold, egg box by egg box, the sleeping visitors in my trap and record their identities and their numbers. All

moths are wonderful, partly because our encounters with them
are so fleeting. In a curious way, using a trap only intensifies these
feelings of mystery, because it helps you to appreciate that moths
are all around but they occupy a parallel world. The moth trap
gives you only momentary access to this completely other place.

I have a special attachment to hawkmoths, not just because
they are the largest and the most beautifully coloured, but also
because there is a kind of quietude about them that many of the
smaller moths don't possess. Often these others fly off the moment
you lift them up on their individual egg box. But hawkmoths rest
sometimes in the exact same spot for twelve hours. The daylong
silence inhabited by these creatures is mysterious too.

At one time, after each morning's count I used to place all my
moths in dense bushes but the garden birds got the hang of that
routine and promptly converted moth beauty into mere moth
mash and avian calories. So now I keep the insects in protective
custody until the following dusk, when they all awake at their
leisure. I love to take the hawkmoths on my fingers up to the last
dregs of light, when their sharp-bristled legs hook to my skin
and create a few moments of ambiguous intimacy. Their wings
quiver intensely to warm the muscles lodged in their thorax so
that they are ready for flight. Then they take off, passing back
once more into the mystery from which they came.

## 21 July 2015

### ⊷ CLAXTON, NORFOLK ⊷

In *The Making of the English Landscape* Hoskins quotes W. H. Hudson
as saying that 18 May is the crown of the British summer. For me
the peak of summer has to have a hairline fracture of rot running
through its real heart and I would locate it at least a couple
of months later. Perhaps a day like today, when the sky was all
December and our thermometer read 25°C. On the horizon low
cloud hung like a deep bog and must have soaked the canopy of

Buckenham woods in its heavy mothering heat. And the rooks, their wings tattered with moult, now rowed across that sky like black paddles through water.

Down the path across the marsh, the grasses swayed high on both sides and the track was a wind-stirred stew of moist air. Now and then I could hear the brittle clatter of Norfolk hawker and brown hawkers' wings as these dragonflies snapped into flight from rest spots in the cleavers and nettle. Whenever I stopped there were notch-horned clegs and deer-flies on my bare arms after a meal. Of all bloodsuckers the latter is among the most beautiful, with its huge eyes of dark opal flecked in orange and green.

It was in contrast to the brooding stillness of the marsh that the hobbies made their impression. The wings are all angled steel, their movements all liquid. The thing I found most fascinating was the way one could infer how they saw the dragonflies from way across the marsh. Then they would cross the intervening pasture of air in flickering wing beats, slowing as they came close and then that sudden upwards surge, wings closing, legs foremost and grappling talons in at the end. Bear in mind that their prey is 1 gram's worth of lightning strike on wings the length of a small bird's: then you start to appreciate the elan of a hunting hobby. Sweeter still was the way the falcons dropped on slow gliding wings to the trenches of still air between the dyke-side vegetation, where the dragonflies themselves were hunting. And the hobbies would sweep into these narrow fissures of stillness and warmth, scooping up prey as they rose back to a sky of dull leaden grey.

## 18 July 2017

### ✂ BLACKWATER, NORFOLK ✂

After explaining to a visitor the lengths I go to encourage marsh and spear thistles on my fen, I was amused to hear her describe the troubles she takes to keep them from her garden. I know they're prickly customers, but why do people dislike thistles?

What I cherish most is the sheer architectural grandeur of the summer plant. Each fully open flowerhead has a kind of declarative beauty – a blend of spine-fringed awkwardness and inner sensuous velvet. No wonder nations have hitched their wagons to the thistle's star-like bloom. Even in autumn, when they are desiccated and devoid of seed floss and possibly enwrapped in old spider's web, thistles retain an aura of dignity.

Yet my real awakening to their virtues was thanks to the bumblebees. I love these insects and they, in turn, adore feeding on thistle blossom. There are few more impressive summer sights in our area than a marsh-thistle bed in a late-June blow. Scores of the magenta-topped spikes bend back and forth in the breeze like some kinetic sculpture. Regardless of this fair-ride movement, the bees cling to those bulbous heads or dance from one swaying wand to another.

My favourite recent visitor to Blackwater's thistles is a leaf-cutting bee called Megachile. It gathers the pollen, but not in a sac on the hind leg as in bumble- or honeybees, rather the stuff is harvested by specialised hairs across the whole underside of its abdomen.

Megachile can swim sometimes for minutes on end through those plush beds in a big spear-thistle head. They also use their legs to press the pollen from the scores of individual florets until they are utterly smothered in the stuff. To watch them about this business, truffling head-first in the plant's sexual parts, one senses that there is an almost ritualised, erotic pattern to the movements. It is as if the insect realises that it's an agent in the thistles' reproduction. There is mutual profit in the process, because more pollinated flowers means more plants next year; and more thistles means more bees. At Blackwater this insect is truly propagator-in-chief in its own garden.

## 19 July 2016

### ⤞ CLAXTON, NORFOLK ⤝

According to the veteran chronicler of English slang Jonathon Green, the expression 'sparrow's-fart' is a late-nineteenth-century coinage, when country folk knew a thing or two about dawns. All I can say is that while Claxton sparrows were busy and loud when I got back to the house, as I left it at 3.55 a.m. they were silent. The early birds were song thrush and blackbird, whose music rose and pooled in the woods beyond the houses and down the dell, by the gate, where the marsh begins.

Under a mauve sky and even with the sun below the rim of the Earth, the summer grasses were already the hue and softness of lion skin stretched across the valley. I judged that I was the only human witness to this square mile. There was a late bat. There were expanding shoals of chironomid midges down the line of the beck. The dew had also drawn out extraordinary numbers of brown or black slugs, which had climbed into the grass canopy to graze, or were too deeply buried in the track's lushness for their own good.

I reached the River Yare when the sun's first effects were a band of exquisite apricot that shaded incrementally colder overhead. Then where it met the edge of the valley it drew an exact charcoal silhouette of Buckenham Carrs, down to the canopy of individual trees. At 4.57 a.m. three spikes of sun flare drove into that dark wood and up levered the entire corona within its orbit of burning white.

In these moments the clouds came to dominate the unfolding drama, because there were flecks of ice-white cirrus in the far northern sky that shone like stars. There was then a closer bank of cumulus battering north, whose advanced line curved like the prow of a ship. While it was lit briefly peach below, there was no colour in the beam but grey. The sun was soon drowned entirely and it occurred to me as I returned to all those chirping birds in another iron-clad Claxton morning that none would guess at the day's real birth.


## 21 July 2014

### ⤞ NORTH RONALDSAY, ORKNEY ⤝

Strange to think that the fulmar once had only a single breeding station in all Britain (St Kilda) until it embarked on a slow expansion around our coasts that has eventually taken it to Kent and Cornwall. It probably arrived at this place in the early twentieth century, where it showed astonishing adaptability. Previously the birds had expressed a preference for sheer cliffs as a nesting location but this low-lying island only rises to 75 feet. Its one striking feature, in fact the largest artefact in all Orkney, is a sea wall (the 'dyke') that bounds the island's entire shore and was built to keep the seaweed-eating ancient sheep off the land and on the rocky beaches. The 180-year-old dyke runs for 12 miles and is now so mottled with the exquisite soft green of sea ivory or the bright orange from Xanthoria lichen that it is a living organism by itself. The dyke represents millions of hours of hard human labour, but to the fulmars it is the most sheltered spot to lay and at intervals in the earth, buttressed at their rear by the dark stone, the parent birds sit patiently on one huge ivory egg or they squat with the oil-filled bag of white fluff that is the growing chick. Together parent and offspring create little pale globes of softness in the dyke's shadow.

The other adults, many of them the mates of the sitting birds or non-breeders, use the dyke as a plaything and alternate a sailing down into the lee of the wall with a sweet rise and turn to catch with perfect timing the uplift of the breeze. Wherever you go these patrolling fulmars cruise back and forth along the line of the dyke, cutting the island's renewed template from the clean air and shaping its character until you cannot think of North Ronaldsay without them. They are the geography of this hard salt-fashioned place turned into feather and air.

## 22 July 2013

As I walk up Peascod (pronounced 'Pusky') Lane at last light the birdsong has dwindled to a handful of voices. It seems appropriate to this phase of the season that they should be either the mechanical repeaters or the sleepy droners, such as the red-legged partridge and its misfiring piston notes or the yellowhammers with their endless rasping phrases.

Then even they fall quiet and I am left to reflect on the way summer has reached a point when all the forward momentum of the season seems to have largely gone. It is as if all that intense and busy flow of life from just a month ago has now become becalmed and is soon to start the inexorable downward journey into that vast delta of colour which we call autumn.

It strikes me that the essence of this moment is perfectly captured in the colour of the grasses that now blanket the field by the lane. Most of them are a species known as Yorkshire fog. The word 'fog' is a little misleading in this context. Originally it was a term for the grass springing up after the hay crop had been taken (incidentally, this second cut of vegetation gave another precise word to the language, because it was also called the 'aftermath'). By chance the suggestion of shimmering mist-laden fields conjured by our more conventional meaning of 'fog' is absolutely true to the softly foaming appearance of this grass species at its ripest. It is a blend of mealy oat white and the rose pink present mainly on the stems but also on a portion of the seed heads. Tonight these shades create the exact same tone as the late sunlight on the thin night clouds. Neither 'orange' nor 'pink' nor 'rose' quite expresses it accurately. It is the exquisite if blurry and ambiguous hue of midsummer. It should perhaps be a colour and a season unto itself: the time of Yorkshire fog.

# AUGUST

⋙ Blackwater Carr, Norfolk ⋘

As I write I have a small canvas bag of yellow rattle seed on my desk. It bulges now like a full purse and the disc-like flattened seeds jangle a little like cash when shuggled about. In fact, if I bought it commercially it would be the equivalent of thirty pounds' worth, which is not bad for two hours' work.

I find it intriguing to discover how a suite of old names once did link yellow rattle to man-made coin. In Somerset it was known simply as 'money' and in Leicestershire as 'money-grass'. I love most, however, a wry Lanarkshire coinage: 'gowk's sixpences' – 'cuckoo's sixpences'. It was probably intended to suggest the idea of fool's gold, but for me it carries a different set of associations.

If not wealth for cuckoos, the flowers are indisputable riches for bumblebees. Behind each single seed imagine the following transaction, repeated hundreds of thousands of times throughout May and June: the insects wandering the flowers relentlessly, pressing down their long tongues into the nectaries, extracting sweetness to grow new bumblebees and, in exchange, dusting the plant stigmas with a few pollen grains from previous blooms. The pollen then germinates and extends a tube down into the plant's ovary where the ovum is fertilised. A month later and we get all that rattling new wealth.

The mutually beneficial relationship between angiosperms and insects dates back to the Cretaceous. So the yellow rattle makes another incidental payout to me in the process: letting me glimpse a fragment of the world once owned by dinosaurs.

Yet the plant's immeasurable donation to this country as a whole was its fundamental place in four million acres of flower-rich meadow. These knee-high forests of insects and colour, flowers and scented hay, were once a glorious centrepiece of the English countryside. Alas in the rush for real cash we lost almost all of them last century. Now just 1 per cent survives. My bag of seed is a small private act of restitution because when sown later this autumn it will expand my embryonic meadow towards its one-acre goal. I know it is not much. Yet it is at least a beginning.

## 4 August 2014

### ⌦ CLAXTON, NORFOLK ⌫

Hen Harrier Day, which is scheduled for next Sunday (10 August), is a radical departure in the story of nature conservation. It comprises a sequence of protest gatherings, most notably at Fairholmes Visitor Centre in the Upper Derwent Valley, but it could just as easily be held at Dersingham Bog in Norfolk. At that site in October 2007 three witnesses, one a Natural England employee, watched as two hen harriers were shot from the sky. No one has yet been charged for that offence.

The unsolved nature of the crime explains the deep frustration felt by many naturalists and some now want an outright ban on driven-grouse shoots. Since 1954 all raptors have been protected by law, but every year the length and breadth of Britain there is a liberal scattering of cases in which landowners, but usually their gamekeepers, are prosecuted for poisoning or shooting peregrines, golden eagles, kites, buzzards, even kestrels and tawny owls. That these are merely the tip of an iceberg is proven by the breeding statistics for hen harriers. Scientific studies conclude that England alone has sufficient habitat for 300 pairs of hen harrier, but this year, like many others, the total will fall abysmally short of that potential. So far 2014 has been a 'good' season, with promise of three breeding pairs.

The reason there are so few is that harriers take grouse chicks and compete with the interests of grouse-moor owners. Driven-grouse shoots rely on the moor holding an unnaturally large surplus of young birds in the late summer in order to justify charges of up to £40,000 for a day's sport. This proliferation – albeit temporary – of one gamebird species has proven to depend on the systematic killing of foxes, crows and every other predator that might possibly interfere with the grouse's success. This year marks a major departure and forty-eight hours before the roar of shotguns spreads across Britain's landed estates, a small group of activists will gather to proclaim peacefully that enough is enough.

4 August 2015

&#x25C4;&#x25C9; BUXTON, DERBYSHIRE &#x25C9;&#x25BA;

Lightwood on the north-western edge of this town is my Ur landscape – the place of sheep-grazed hills, steep-sided cloughs and rushing water over dark gritstone beds that launched my relationship with the whole of nature. Sadly it has also become a landscape of loss, since many of my most treasured fixtures – lapwing, woodcock, grey partridge, ring ouzel, tree pipit and wood warbler – have now all gone.

Yet recently I was delighted to find that Lightwood has also gained since my childhood. As we walked along the track where the old reservoir has been drained and dismantled we were shocked to find both sides smothered in tangled banks of marsh bedstraw, ragged robin, valerian, marsh thistle, greater bird's-foot trefoil, tormentil and, here and there, great phallic spikes of spotted orchid. On the higher slopes were patches of bilberry already with fruit and swaying passionately in the breeze were the magenta-headed columns of foxglove.

Why was all this glorious colour here now when I had never known it in my early days? Then the penny dropped. Based on the young birch and alder saplings that are springing up, I can infer that at some point in the last decade the sheep have been taken off all these slopes. What had once been shorn turf sprinkled with the yellow studs of tormentil has become a garden and an incipient wood. It is a perfect expression of the rewilding presently championed by George Monbiot in his book *Feral*.

Then we stumbled on the crowning motif for this new riff in Lightwood's ongoing song. There nestled among the grasses was a dark green fritillary butterfly, the first I've seen here in more than half a century. The species does occur in Derbyshire but at headline sites like Dove Dale. The cold morning had momentarily immobilised the creature and it lay on its side so that we could not see the tiger-coloured wings with their broken transverse ripples of black. Now we had to make do with only the underwing: an oval of faintly iridescent moss green banded in straw yellow and studded with twenty-one silver-white 'eyes'.

### 16 August 2016

#### ❧ CLAXTON, NORFOLK ☙

My summer's highlight, as we sit in the garden most evenings, has been to watch the pre-migration flocking behaviour of our village swifts. No one knows what purpose it serves, but it is thought to play some role in flock cohesion. At its height up to thirty birds were involved and all were crushed into a ravelling ball of anarchy burning across the heavens. I find it all the more magnificent to know that the whole ecology of this behaviour, even the species itself, is based entirely on insects, but converted to swift speed and scream.

Like the flock I circle around and around, but no fishing net of words seems to catch it. Could one possibly express it better as a taste rather than as any visual sensation? It is like red chilli crushed into a gloop of honey; the essence of all the Americas mingled with that from all Africa and Eurasia; a taste perhaps of Pangaea.

More than the flock, what has touched me most is that, after all the other swifts migrated, a single pair is still feeding young. Their chicks must be late and the parents have lingered and one cannot help but wonder – agonise really – how it feels to be left behind after all that oneness.

The sky is now running still over Claxton but for a while I have these singletons above our garden. There's something curiously inelegant, almost clumsy, in the way that swifts fly. The wings working hard, gaffing the air, blunt-edged paddles wobbling hopelessly and then – because it's all part of swift treachery – out of this pantomime of effort comes that sweep away, beyond the range of my eye, and back into view, hard over the village green and in one long glide. Bang! Into the mole hole at the roof's edge.

Surely more than anything else in British nature, swifts symbolise all of life and it is all here now in the line of that curve. It has the certainty of a steel blade. It is shaped like a strand of cobweb weighted with dew. It has the line of the Earth's own rim mid-ocean and a memory of it hangs momentarily in the air like breath on a winter's morning.

## 18 August 2014

### ◄ BLACKWATER CARR, NORFOLK ►

One cannot call it autumn, perhaps, but there is a moment in early August when the year begins its next metamorphosis. Summer seems to sclerotise and in the breeze the leaves begin to sound brittle; you notice that the flowers are steadily more magenta than yellow, and then there are suddenly the dragonflies. This remarkable increase among our largest insects is a definite waymarker of seasonal change. On the approach to my patch there are dozens of them, mainly common darters, brown and migrant hawkers, luxuriating in a tunnel of hot air cut through the vegetation by the track.

Yet the highlight was a southern hawker in the wood by the gate. Unlike the other species, this one often cleaves to the edge of woods. The male hawker patrolled a longitudinal tunnel of shadow above a dyke but he mainly kept to the cave mouth – so to speak – darting out of the gloom into the wider shoals of light, up the bank and across the track where I stood to watch. The lattice pattern of sunshine falling through the poplar leaves overhead meant that the acid-green stripes in his abdomen glowed momentarily golden as he explored the shoreline to his patch.

His powers of flight have a heritage spanning more than 300 million years and he arced through three planes of space so smoothly that he could turn faster than the human eye could follow. Binoculars were useless. I saw the insect less as a whole organism, and more as an occasional blur, a momentary pattern, a glittering inference. It was as if we inhabited different atmospheres. Where I wallowed in air, he passed through something finer and lighter. Yet if reminiscent of anything, his twisting fish-like motion back and forth suggested something sub-aquatic and predatory. When he interspersed those deft quick turns with a slower split-second ellipse there was in that curving moment, before he vanished back into his cave, the unmistakable image of a shark.

18 August 2015

Claxton, Norfolk

Summertime and the living is easy in our garden, except if you happen to feed on earthworms. Then the withered lawn and parched earth of August drive a number of our neighbours to take special measures. The most conspicuous indicator of summer drought is a bit of avian behaviour that's more often heard than seen.

It results in a small hollow hammering noise of shell on stone and, aside from the wider hush enveloping our flowerbeds, you could easily overlook its quiet rhythmic tap. Yet a song thrush at its anvil is as redolent of Claxton at this particular moment in summer as the bell-like notes of full-blown song on late July evenings. I'm guessing it is largely a hedge-bottom business, because the snails themselves also collect in those shaded, damper conditions beneath the brambles, but I also wonder whether there is another factor at play.

When he was a post-doctorate student at Oxford and before *Zoo Time* (1956) went on air or *The Naked Ape* (1967) was written, the immensely versatile Desmond Morris published a paper on snail-eating thrushes. Now sixty-one years old, it was a very thorough piece of work because it is still cited as a key document on the subject. Morris showed that the 'anvil' was not a stone selected by tradition or habit, but for its geographical proximity to where the snails were first caught. He also showed that the hammering action involved the thrush holding its prey by the shell lip or the flesh, and that successful breakage was followed by a bill-wiping phase to clean away the slime and shell fragments.

Morris's other revelation, which contradicted earlier ornithologists including the great Victorian authority William Yarell, was that blackbirds lacked the necessary coordination and 'nervous equipment' to master this snail-breaking technique. But they have found a way to enjoy the savour of freshly cracked mollusc. They sit, wait and watch, then steal them off their smarter but smaller song thrush relatives. I surmise that this piracy, which is known technically as kleptoparasitism, explains why our song thrushes are as keen on the shaded seclusion of the hedge bottom as they are on snail flesh itself.

19 August 2013

~~~ CLAXTON, NORFOLK ~~~

For weeks now the inspection of my moth trap has been a complicated business. As I pull out the egg boxes in which my invertebrate charges sleep, a robin has tried to do a little moth inspection of its own. It is the tattiest bird you've ever seen with just two tail feathers and an orange bib that's full of 'moth holes'. The sparse covering over the belly and back sticks out at odd angles as if the plumes are about to fall out and instead of a sleek sprite it looks like an animated feather duster.

Yet it reminds us of the great drama in the birds' year that humans invariably fail to notice – moult. At the close of the breeding season, resident species such as robins drop their entire plumage and acquire a fresh one. Without this renewal they could not survive the rigours of winter. It is moult that explains why almost every gull you see presently has a wedge-shaped gap along the hindwing where they lose the inner primaries. It's also why the rooks and jackdaws round us are so dishevelled that sometimes one wonders how they fly at all.

During this phase birds that were previously conspicuous suddenly fall silent and almost disappear. Yet everyone has witnessed moult, if only subliminally, because any body of water, especially the park lake or village pond, has its surface film of summer dust topped by a flotilla of free-floating feathers that wander to the water's edge and gather like tiny robin-sized boats.

Many of these come from ducks that go into a special dowdy plumage phase known as 'eclipse' when they drop all the vital flight feathers. Moult is most obvious when it's over, because it's then that robins resume their poignant autumn song. It is also when we notice the male mallards with those emerald heads glittering like polished stone and which look as if they've emerged fresh minted from some feather-soft furnace of life.

### 29 August 2017

### CLAXTON, NORFOLK

The view from my office includes a junction box where five telephone wires converge at the top of a pole. For several years it has been a favourite gathering place for the season's young swallows and they wreath this banal technology in the joyous rhythms of their movement and sound.

The immatures are separable by pale fringes to the wing feathers, but also by downturned yellow gape-lines at the corners of their mouths, which give them a wonderfully comic, clown-like glumness. It is as if all the swirl of these late-August days – the balletic fly-snatching, the sun-blessed leisure, the quiet feather care as they sit amid a pool of the adult swallows' desultory song – were a source of strange ennui.

Eventually scores of them have crowded on to this temporary maypole and I can study the minutiae of their collective lives: the way they exercise and stretch full-tailed to expose eye spots on each plume; the way they preen or nibble their underwings to discipline stray feathers, or bury their heads, beak-in-back, and snooze for a second or two before resuming the various tasks.

Occasionally a newcomer lands badly and then he shuffles and flutters to align his feather weight to the wire. If I draw my focus back a fraction to take them all in I can see how, at any moment, their individual actions rock the lines and each bird must readjust to the wave-like pulses of movement, flicking tail feathers up and down and collectively riding out the tide swell of air, before they settle back to a sort of stillness.

There is, however, danger in all this tranquillity. Several times a day a sparrowhawk or hobby churns up the birdlife of Claxton and starlings and pigeons and goldfinches also suddenly rise and as the predators cross the village one can mark their trajectory in a radar of swallow notes, the intensity of calls – *swee-swee-swee* – sculpting their lines of exit. Then swallows come back to my pole and wires, calm settling over the earlier dread like falling snow, and blue birds clothe bare lines in a renewed vision of old summer.

# SEPTEMBER

I September 2013

‹ CLAXTON, NORFOLK ›

I suspect it's often overlooked that the most silent of the British seasons is not winter but summer, and especially that late-summer spell as the school holidays come to a close. It was so without sound as we walked our routine circuit through the local lanes that it was almost unnerving. It was as if a great, as yet undisclosed, absence had come to dwell there and was growing somewhere among the sunlit trees and those stubble fields that are now the exact colour of lion skin.

One glorious effect of this wider silence is its capacity to emphasise the one sound that can be heard now in every local hedge or field – the songs of grasshoppers and bush crickets. In one short walk I heard Roesel's and dark bush crickets as well as three species of grasshopper. The commonest of the five – abundant even among the desiccated ragwort and oat grass of our lawn edge – is the field grasshopper. The male's song is a terse dry purr that he repeats at short intervals, the gaps becoming progressively shorter if the larger female is present to inspire his music. In fact, just before the moment of physical contact it can spill over completely into an intense structureless orgy of buzzing notes.

There is about all this courtship a bass note of humour, partly because of that long-jawed goat-like sadness that is so evident in grasshopper faces and partly because their love-making is so gauche while their urges are so directly expressed. He shows immense patience as he performs his simple coarse-grained song for her, yet once she gives the secret signal for copulation he leaps aloft with lightning speed. Occasionally some interloping male will also mount that same broad female back and then all three organisms, in a confusing tangle of antennae, wings and eighteen bristle-haired limbs will wander from view, into that wider Eden of grass root and soil crumb that is a grasshopper's world.


1 September 2014

⊷ BLACKWATER CARR, NORFOLK ⊶

It was there beside me in the vegetation while I was photographing flowers, but it took me minutes to spot it. Then in one pulse of acuity its extraordinariness ravelled up into conscious recognition. An exquisite latticework of black lines was wrapped around a soft three-inch tube of khaki green. The fractured pattern, like shattered glass or silk webbing, had earlier harmonised with the interplay of light, shadow and the hundred vertical lines of plant stems. Now it stared at me, silver eyes glowing, as an elephant hawkmoth caterpillar. The odd name derives from the trunk-like structure at the creature's anterior end. Those 'eyes', four of them in total, are actually warning spots placed behind the mouthparts, which create the illusion of all-seeing vigilance and help deter possible predators.

Perhaps it was the dramatic way that the creature revealed itself that made it seem miraculous. Yet there is also the thought that this animal, while seeming so clearly structured, will soon wander off and wrap itself within the hardened case of its cocoon. Then imagine that this soft sac of body parts will dissolve steadily through the winter into a soup of protein, only to emerge next spring as an entirely different beast: a large moth with beautifully patterned wings of ginger and lipstick pink.

One must also factor in the reflection that the willowherb plant supplying all the caterpillar's nutrients was just a pale shoot emerging from the peat this spring. Now it stands almost five feet tall and is studded with magenta flowers not too unlike the colour of the adult hawkmoth. Through this plant's ancient trick of photosynthesis the great hairy willowherb performs a radical transformation of its own, consuming light and turning it into carbohydrates plus waste oxygen. In a sense, by spotting a caterpillar I can appreciate two forms of metamorphosis. Strange, really, to realise that life's three-billion-year-long heritage is there in that patch by the track.

## 1 September 2015

### ⤐ CLAXTON, NORFOLK ⤏

It is perhaps the strangest wildlife alarm ever to be heard in our house. It began when our daughter, at 3 a.m. outside our bedroom door and shrouded in her duvet (to stop it getting tangled in her hair, she later revealed!), announced that there was a bat in her room.

Sure enough there was the improbable and rather forlorn vision of a medium-sized species, perhaps a brown long-eared bat or a Daubenton's bat, circling the lamp-lit rectangle of space just above her bed. Its flight path was necessarily short and repetitive. In fact, it reminded me of one of those black ragged props, popular in low-budget vampire movies of the fifties, that used to circle on wires before the victim's blood was spilt.

What followed was definitely a show of two halves. One of the mammals, armed with a short-handled butterfly net, flailed hopelessly at the ceiling each time the bat passed. Despite the metronomic regularity of the bat's circuit not one of these fifty-plus net swipes came remotely close to fulfilling its intended purpose. (And the increasingly hysterical laughter from the main actor didn't help the performance either!)

If one sets aside the bat's initial error in entering the bedroom (but also the mystery of how and why), what struck me was the extraordinary dexterity of its flight. What was most impressive about this encounter was the way that the bat, micro-second by micro-second, sculpted the entire interior space of that room through bouncing ultrasonic calls off all the objects present, including the frantic idiot with the butterfly net, and then processed the rebounded echoes as an interior map of its physical surroundings. In effect the creature avoided all attempts at capture through 'hearing' the whole scene. The evolution of echo-location, by which this mammal family moves, hunts, feeds and has its being, has never seemed more miraculous.

Then it performed its final trick. The bat fired pulses of sound at the windows and eventually discovered a small change in the pattern (when the human recovered sufficient gumption to open them) and through that slit of darkness this wonderful little sound artist flew out into the sanctity of deep night.

5 September 2017

>—❦ MONIACK MHOR ❦—<

Aside from the slurry of S sounds tipped out by a roadside burn, there was nothing at this spot but the early-morning hush of the moor. Yet the silence seemed only to emphasise all the internal noise generated in me by an assault from the ravenous midges. They started as a loose-meshed veil about my hands and face but soon thickened into a maddening private halo. They particularly wanted my wrists – I have twenty-three spots there as I type these words – and I could invert my binoculars to watch the 2-millimetre beasts, with their pin-thin heads and barred bodies, at their minute works. How can something so easily turned to a smudgy dot on the notebook page puncture human skin?

Yet in many ways it was this incessant swarm that said most about the arresting impact of those spiders' webs. Despite my midge cloud I instantly jammed on the brakes and pushed the bike over the verge, reaching for the binoculars and camera. Looking out over about a hectare of wet ground, I tried to calculate the spider numbers and in one 4-metre square I counted about ninety webs. Yet other parts were almost twice as densely covered and in places the forest canopy of thistle, ling, scabious and soft rush was sunk in a near-weightless empire of silk.

It was mainly the work of hammock weavers, which don't produce the symmetrical spheres of orb-weavers. Tight-meshed layers of silk had been suspended mid-air and from that the spiders had then spun irregular connective shrouds that bound the web to multiple anchors in the bog vegetation. 'Hammock' nicely describes many of the concave structures – except that their owners hang upside down beneath their 'couch' – but there were also Christmas-tree-shaped tents draped around spikes of rush.

I wondered if this entire scintillation could be the work of a single genetic community: one spider clan, perhaps, by a burn. I also pondered what they awaited to enmesh in all this thread work, and slowly it dawned that this whole shimmering landscape – the spiders, the silk, even the swallows and wagtails undulating overhead, since they must surely eat them as well – was here, unlike me, precisely because the midges were present in such abundance.

## 14 September 2016

### ⤞ NORWICH ⤝

It was one of the more uplifting talks I have ever given. There I was, microphone in hand, braced against the January cold and with an al fresco audience of fifty hardy souls by the broad at the University of East Anglia. Suddenly there was a ripple of *oohs* and *aahs* coming from the assembled crowd, but – alas – it was not an approving response to my words. It was for an otter that had completely upstaged me.

Just as I was talking this wonderful creature had surfaced in the broad directly behind and my speech was rapidly suspended while we all took in this extraordinary coincidence. Next day it even made the front pages of the *Eastern Daily Press*.

And well it deserved to; sightings of them are not everyday occurrences. But the vision of one while you are actually opening the guided walk really could not be more eloquent. As the otter announced, the University of East Anglia truly is wonderful for wildlife.

Dr Iain Barr, senior lecturer in the school of biological sciences, has been part of a team that has assembled an inventory of wildlife in the surrounding grounds and adjacent Eaton Park. To date it stands at 5,500 species, which ranks it among the best in the region. It is more species, for example, than at The Lodge, headquarters for the Royal Society for the Protection of Birds. Among university campuses it must be the most biodiverse in Britain. What a fabulous asset for a place of learning!

Of moths alone Iain and his colleagues have recorded more than 900 species, which represents almost 40 per cent of the entire British total. The site also has twenty-three varieties of dragonfly, more than some of the best wildlife reserves in the Broads. It holds not just otters but also water voles, water rails, bearded tits and bitterns.

A major change I have noticed since I attended the university in the 1980s is the enhanced management of the surrounding grassland. In my day, for some inexplicable reason, it was mown to within an inch of its life as if we were all still on a golf course. The wildlife value of those 'greens' was virtually nil.

Go today, however, and there is a network of cut trails around the site for the convenience of myriad walkers, runners and picnickers, but the rest of the vegetation is tall, lush and full of wild flowers and insects.

In a matter of minutes I was immersed in the reeling songs of Roesel's bush crickets and those of a delightfully named relative, the long-winged conehead. Neither insect was ever recorded in Norfolk until 1997 and the presence of both is a measure of UEA's improving value for nature.

One other classic indicator of the importance of these grasslands is on the other side of the river, closer to the Science Park. That zone had 207 bee orchid spikes this spring and now the rarer pyramidal orchid has also been found. In autumn it holds a range of mushrooms known as waxcaps. This group are often bright-topped fungi and lovers of old grassland and the presence of eleven species suggests that the area could have been managed in the same way for a very long time.

Given that we have lost 99 per cent of our best grassland areas in this country and given that it is unusual even to report on a site that is improving rather than declining in value, it comes as a shock to learn that all is now threatened by the development of a 300-vehicle car park scheduled for construction by Norwich Rugby Club on university land.

The development is bizarre given the UEA's worldwide reputation for research on climate change and its own commitments to a sustainable future, working, as it proclaims on its own website, 'to reduce negative environmental impacts' and on the creation of a low-carbon campus.

Equally troubling is the effect of building a large car park and floodlit AstroTurf pitches on the area's role as a wildlife corridor. Iain Barr explains the issue in the context of the bats, which he has surveyed all over Norwich. 'We have eleven species here at the UEA, which is excellent in itself, but if you look at a map of the city and its surrounding areas those records are clustered along the two rivers, the Wensum and the Yare.

'It means that the river here at the UEA functions,' he continues, 'like a wildlife highway right into the heart of our city in a way that happens in very few built-up areas in Britain. And it is not just about the bats, many of which are rare themselves. The bats are there because it is great for insects. And the insects are there because it is great for vegetation – the diverse wild plants and trees, etc. It is an entire wild network right in the densest, most populated part of our county. It is astonishing and we should all be proud and work to protect it. Not to damage it.'

As you walk around the UEA grounds you are struck by its daily usage by so many people – dog walkers, strollers, joggers, etc. – who are probably only subliminally aware that this green space is also wonderful for nature. Yet that doesn't diminish its importance. It increases it. It means that we and 5,500 other species are all in one place together. Norwich and its university, surely, should work to keep it that way.

15 September 2014

CLAXTON, NORFOLK

It's well documented that hobbies are the only falcons with the speed and agility to catch swifts and swallows on the wing. Yet in forty-three years I've never seen it. I once saw a hobby flail down among sand martins over Cley Marshes and scatter them like a gust through loose feathers. I once saw a merlin above Burgh Castle spiral in a relentless tight corkscrew as it pursued a skylark that steepled up until it was only a dust mote.

Such failed efforts, which are themselves rarely seen, put in context what I experienced recently. A neighbour and I stood on our drive chatting, when a hobby breezed down metres from us and lunged at several perched hirundines. All through the last month these beautiful migrants have been threaded down the wires and brought colour and music to the heart of our village. Occasionally they give me notice of passing predators, when the slurred chatter of house martins swells in panic and the swallows make intense, repeated *fe-swee* notes and spear outwards, flip-flopping side to side as they go.

Somehow this hobby gave no warning. It angled and twisted, talons probing down on a swallow. Still it failed and off it flew, circling away. The martins and swallows fizzed out until the September stillness quieted their nerves once more. Then from nowhere it burst back among us. The swallow with its back to the approach can have had no fear, until the moment it was plucked from the wire. My friend had never seen a hobby before ever and I wondered, as the whole village leant in upon itself towards this moment, what each of us took from it. I remember most vividly, as the prey was seized, how one lazuline wing fell outwards like a flag; the hobby's wings seemed to chop and paddle and there was this momentary drama-less inelegance to it, then the falcon swept the victim back into the peerless symmetry of its going, and all was done.

## 15 September 2015

### ❧ CLAXTON, NORFOLK ❧

It seems apt that mushrooms are made from the same stuff as insects – chitin – because, like insects, they have a gift for sudden unexpected appearance. One moment nothing, then, as if on wings, they descend everywhere. We must acknowledge that this fungal sense of the dramatic relies partly on us. We simply fail to notice something so lowly, so brown, so inhuman, and yet so fundamental to life, until it does something eye-catching.

In our garden the best display has been mounted on the back lawn. Despite a fey hint of Gallic artistry or culinary sophistication in the name – and they are said to be delicious – some of these fairy ring champignons look like small crumpled turds. The one undeniable flourish in their appearance is the rough circle they have inscribed on the grass. What I find just as compelling is the way that the lawn is so much greener precisely where they have reared their mouldy heads.

I can infer the organism's subterranean habits from the appearance of those fruiting bodies – the mushrooms themselves – and from the fresher colour in the lawn. In that lightless place the main organism, known as the mycelium, is entwined with filaments that are finer than spun silk. A single fibre, known as a hypha, is one hundredth of a millimetre thick. Yet in a single kilogram of woodland soil there can be 200 kilometres of hyphae and underneath an entire wood there will be millions of kilometres of these living pathways. There they traffic in nutrients, processing the hard lignin and resistant woody tissues – and annually five tonnes of this vegetable junk is dumped per hectare – and converting it into elements that the trees and flowers can re-use. That orbit of green in the middle of our lawn is a result of the nitrogen processed by fairy-ring champignons.

That circle of colour speaks truly of the underworld. Some fungi are treacherous, some are highly destructive, and some even deadly poisonous. We often clothe their names in images of Hadean darkness, yet they are the black stuff that, come spring, helps bring Persephone's radiance to all our lives.

## 16 September 2013

### ⤙ CLAXTON, NORFOLK ⤚

It's hard to say which was more unpleasant: the bruising grind of a JCB as its immense orange limb lugged up bucket after bucket full of slub from the dyke. Or was it the foul envelope of hydrogen sulphide that cloaked me when the black slurry was pitched on to the field edge. Yet even this workaday scene had its inner eye of grace.

As I passed the machine amid its task, a grey heron launched itself unwillingly and ploughed off, its breastbone resting heavy on the damp autumn air. I had barely moved away before it was back, landing with an awkward flourish, and then it stalked forward all angles and knock-kneed and cross-eyed, the neck writhing skywards, until it resumed once more its little hunched pocket of silence and poise by the heap of mud. I love the way that herons home in with such speed on these man-made feeding opportunities. Birds have been found fishing at night under the glow of sodium lamps, or they routinely poach garden ponds for carp, and can follow the plough or the combine, picking off prey as it escapes the larger human predators.

There was a time in Claxton when the opportunism was the other way round. The Norfolk scholar Sir Thomas Browne described in the seventeenth century how spoonbills, which once bred in our village, were harvested, the young being gathered and caged and fed on garbage until they were fat enough for the table. How times change. For once these long-legged birds offer us small signs of hope in a troubled landscape. Little egrets are now on the brink of breeding abundance, while cattle and great white egrets, with little bitterns and purple herons, are all prospecting their first British nest sites. Better still is the establishment of a small breeding colony of spoonbills on the north Norfolk coast, which involved at least nine pairs raising fourteen young in 2011 and was the first substantial breeding record for over 330 years.

## 17 September 2012

### ⤟ CLAXTON, NORFOLK ⤠

This year we've derived immense pleasure from the butterflies that have clothed our garden buddleia in brilliance during the late summer. Even as they grace us with these brief gifts I've tried to think of any creatures or plants that are more lovely. My list was pretty short. I came up with some bird families, such as the hummingbirds, the Asiatic pheasants (and other gamebirds) and birds-of-paradise. Then there are coral reefs with their rainbow shoals of tropical fish, but who has more than occasional opportunities to enjoy them? The only competition close to home is probably flower-rich meadows (whose own enchantment, it should be said, invariably entails the presence of so many butterflies). We must also acknowledge that this is now largely an experience reserved for continental Europe, given how much the British have opted to forgo this habitat. (We've lost more than 99 per cent in this country.)

Yet it also occurred to me while watching this year's buddleia that there are actually two types of lepidopteran beauty on display. The creatures which highlighted the issue were the red admirals, those predominantly black-winged insects with a hot hoop of Carboniferous crimson stamped across the entire upper surface. When the wings fold up and the red hemispheres are hidden below the underwing, a much stranger and less accessible aesthetic experience is ours.

From any distance the underside is superficially like a rather mouldy old leaf. Yet look closer and it resolves into an exquisitely complex marbling or a mosaic of muted turquoise and yellow. There are then little islands of brown inked around with thick black lines, successive waves of burgundy or blue, whose jagged curves resemble those strands of flotsam dumped by the tide at the sea edge. It's a world of colour that masquerades as dead vegetation. It is also a beauty wholly distinct from the flaming colours of the upper wing and its main purpose is to disguise that other form of beauty from us.

18 September 2014

NORWICH

I saw a miracle the other day. It was balanced on a wire by the house. It was a swallow, which bore those pale flanges at its beak edges that are the telltale marks of a young bird. The downturned gape gave its facial expression such a wonderful aura of innocence, but don't be fooled.

It looks cute, but that enamel-blue bird is made of something tougher than steel. Very soon it will follow its instincts south over the English Channel, down through France and Spain and across the Straits of Gibraltar. In a single non-stop odyssey it will then traverse the greatest desert on Earth.

Perhaps it will linger over the camel thorn of the Sahel region, but as the drab mists creep over the Norfolk landscape, our village swallow will swoop and play in the humid insect-rich updraughts above the Congo rainforest. In advance of Christmas it will cross the entire length of Angola, possibly also Namibia, before swinging east to pass our winter in the summer sunlight of South Africa. Come February it will begin the whole journey in reverse and be back in our village by April.

The direct linear distance is *just* 12,000 miles but who knows what total mileage the bird will cover in its meandering course? When I see it again that young swallow may have flown 30,000–40,000 miles, more than the circumference of the whole planet. It weighs about an ounce.

Swallow species of various kinds have long been favourites for much of humanity. One factor in our affections is self-interest. Swallows must be the most beautiful and the most environmentally friendly insecticide on Earth. These birds love to eat the creatures that we often like the least. It is an established fact that flies, cow dung, green grass, cattle, barns and swallows are all elements in an ecological whole.

Yet the bird's powerful symbolism for most of humanity transcends mere diet. Swallows partake of one of the most magical colours in all nature: blue. Almost all blue birds are much loved or are culturally important. One thinks in Britain of the kingfisher and blue tit, but these examples only hint at the colour's wider impact. Among birds-of-paradise, the one most sought after is the blue bird-of-paradise. Of parrots, the most desired, financially valued and now the most controversial have the same captivating hue. They are the Lear's and Spix's Macaw, which have both been relentlessly hunted and collected for the cage-bird trade until they teeter on the edge of extinction.

Blue is such a strangely contradictory colour that it is difficult to formulate a simple sense of its psychological impact. On the one hand it is the colour of depression, sadness and of the outsider, most famously captured in the glorious music of the black community in the American Deep South. The Blues was a music of consolation but also of protest. Equally one could name the radical associations in the most famous paintings of Picasso's monumental oeuvre – his 'Blue Period'.

On the other hand, blue is the colour of faith, tradition, law and order, the military, the police and officialdom. It is, for example, the chromatic insignia of the Conservative Party, which champions many of the qualities or elements listed above.

Recently I was able to observe how the blueness of swallows, as well as their migratory habits, has come to carry powerful associations for one modern European community. In Estonia this summer I learnt that the Baltic country has chosen the swallow as a national emblem. The bird's plumage is mirrored even in the blue, white and black of their flag.

Estonia may be among the most successful, democratic and forward-looking of the recently liberated Soviet states, yet the country has a tragic past, having endured centuries of oppression from Scandinavian conquerors, German landowners and, latterly, from Russian communist apparatchiks. One can see why the swallow would be so appealing to this long-suffering people. Throughout their darkest period (represented by the black on their flag), the Estonians kept faith (symbolised by the blue) that the migrant bird of hope would one day return to see them liberated.

This summer I also came across a very different if equally modern swallow symbolism when I visited the Orkneys. Several crofters told me how they had never known breeding swallows in their childhood, but today the birds are widespread throughout the islands. This extension northwards is a measure of the warming conditions that are being induced by climate change.

Conversely, the swallow populations of south-eastern England are now being hollowed out, probably because of persistent agro-chemical usage and the loss of dairy farming from our region, as well as the disappearance of the vernacular architecture in which they love to nest. The overall effect of these changes is that British swallows are trending northwards.

All of this reflects how the young swallow I saw near our house was more than a miracle. On its gentle blue back this creature carries a whole story about human experience.

We should cherish swallows for what they gift to us and for what they tell us about ourselves.

## 19 September 2017

### ⤳ CLAXTON, NORFOLK ⤝

I saw them as I went to the bin. In the web of a female garden cross spider, a worker common carder bee hung upside down. The two were plainly engaged in combat and I crouched to observe the drama more closely.

Yet there were more emotions at play in this encounter than mere curiosity. For while I admire spiders, I absolutely love bumblebees. To see this insect so enmeshed and at risk of being eaten required an effort of will by me not to intervene. In his gloriously funny book *The Spider* John Crompton admitted that he freed bees from webs without further ado.

It is hard not to share his instinct that these contests entail a personal moral issue. Yet if we cannot help but anthropomorphise, perhaps we should process that while the bee is a dutiful, hardworking, socially minded daughter, equally the spider is probably a loyal mother pursuing her natural trade. And just as one pollinates my beans, the other will spare our house from late-summer's fly menace.

I must admit there was a third powerful charge at work near that bin. For if I admire spiders, I also fear them. I may have never shown the kind of distressing paralysis that would overcome my poor arachnophobic mother, but I have known moments of delicious horror: the time a four-inch solifugid crossed the floor of a Moroccan hut towards me; the occasion a tarantula emerged in slow motion from bananas on our Amazonian canoe; then the morning a huge huntsman lazed directly over my Queensland bed.

In his excellent new book, *The Animals Among Us*, John Bradshaw suggests that we share the same reflexes towards venomous spiders and snakes as many of our primate relatives.

Humans are genetically programmed to detect spider outlines rapidly. The system is located in the pulvinar neurons, which fire information from the retina to the fear-inducing areas of the brain called the amygdala.

It is remarkable to reflect that englobed in this startling morning moment by the waste bin is not only an invertebrate contest as old as the Cretaceous, but also something of my own species' 100,000-year-old story on Earth.

20 September 2016

BLACKWATER, NORFOLK

At present it's almost impossible to walk the rides around my patch and not snap spiders' silk. It is everywhere. I notice, as I drive over to Blackwater, that there are even webs on both wing mirrors but, with the sun at the right angle, you can see that there is barely a twig or leaf not bound with gossamer to its neighbours.

Those threads are, gram for gram, five times stronger than steel. Yet the thing that strikes me most is not the strength but the elasticity of spider's web. I was watching how that of a female garden cross spider had just snared a honeybee (an unusual prey at Blackwater, although wasps are commonplace) and while the victim whirred its wings or pulsed the abdomen to break free, the web yawed but held true. It is remarkable to watch spiders at work in these encounters: the extreme caution, the delicate octave of their movements and then the certainty with which they manipulate the insect and inexorably mummify it with silk.

I know this scenario reverses the usual moral order humans plonk on top of nature but spiders need love too and garden cross spiders must be among September's most beautiful stars. They are so gloriously varied, from a chaste grey studded with the usual white cruciform right through to oiled mahogany inlaid with cream.

One indisputable merit to this brief arachnid empire is the way that all those shining threads turn even our worst works – and I'm thinking of the lifeless gardens in many surrounding villages of wall-like leylandii and lawns shorn to look like pool tables – into multiple sheets of dewed silver. The desert is made momentarily fertile. One estimate of abundance, a million spiders an acre in some habitats, implies billions of miles of this crystallised protein. Recall that since flies are the main arachnid prey, we really owe much of this whole show of silk and sunshine to a group of insects that is often more reviled than their captors. It may be powered by flies but spiders are the key agents and they have now clothed our entire landscape in a single garment: all Britain, perhaps, as one glittering weave.

## 29 September 2014

### ✎ BLACKWATER CARR, NORFOLK ✎

One thing I've learnt from my patch is that managing habitat for wildlife is not so much a plan implemented as a prayer offered. And this prayer cost much sweat. For weeks I heaved sodden vegetation, forkful by forkful and barrow-load by barrow-load, on to what's known in our household as 'Slub Mountain' (or, worse, 'Pater's Folly'). It's a mound of nutrient-rich waste that had previously been hauled out the dyke or cut from the reed. At times it stood 8 feet tall but this has gradually rotted down to a heap that is chest high. It's a paradise for those small, dark, ground-scuttling arachnids called wolf spiders. Occasionally a red admiral rests on its sunny slopes. But for long months there was not the faintest trace of its intended occupant.

Last week I glanced as usual in its direction and there, coiled on the crown, was the answer to a prayer. I love the way grass snakes move: that effortless pouring forward in sinuous if diminishing lines. That slow going away to nothing but the tail tip: it feels less like a willed motion than an involuntary process.

This one was sucked steadily into the ground like a brief gutter of dark water emptied by force of gravity. I went back often to repeat the encounter. Sometimes I could almost touch her before she leaves. Then I found her shed skin shining on the top.

The dorsal scales are oval and diaphanous and look like the popped cells in bubble wrap. The belly scales feel like overlapping pieces of old dried Sellotape that have lost adhesion. Through this mysterious act of renewal (technically called ecdysis) a new snake emerges head first from its old self. I am left only with a ghost, but I touch the slender tube, rustling like plastic, and think of the ground it slithered over, the water it breasted and the male snake that coiled around it. I reflect on the swelling womb that once lay within it, nourished by the sunlight, that caused her to answer my prayer and mount that soft-soiled hill to breed.

29 September 2015

CLAXTON, NORFOLK

In this slow-draining delta of colour that we name 'autumn' I think the most beautiful thing I have seen this year is a holly hedge at Walcot Hall, Shropshire, entirely meshed with spider's webs. And in that morning light they were scattered over with dew. Spiders claim September like no other month, but spare a thought, perhaps, for male spiders since these days are also most treacherous.

In the nettle bed by the dyke I came across one hopeful male on the edge of an orb-web spun by a particularly grand garden cross spider. The latter had just trussed up her latest catch, a wasp, and was laying her forelegs over that still-living insect in readiness to dissolve it with her digestive juices. Even this scene needs a brief gloss, because in these encounters arachnids don't have it all their own way. Earlier on the path I'd watched a worker wasp deliberately land in another web and force its owner to drop to the foliage below. The wasp then hauled at a partly digested fly at the centre until the silk strands holding it, which were stronger gram for gram than steel cable, snapped finally and the insect flew away with a spider's meal. This second wasp was not so lucky and her long aristocratic jaws and black oval eyes were immobilised beneath a pall of silk.

The only thing that delayed its death was the male spider proceeding cautiously towards the female. He fingered her silk orb and then with his long slender limbs reached out towards a potential mate, who was perhaps six times heavier. Alas she was as aggressive towards her would-be suitor as she was towards the wasp. Only one urge was to be satisfied on this occasion. In some species four of ten male spiders are eaten by the females. But give a final thought to the male redback spiders that actually perform a suicidal sex jump into their mate's waiting jaws. By copulating and simultaneously feeding her cannibalistic urges, he fulfils his ultimate genetic destiny but also gives nourishment to the mother of his offspring.

# OCTOBER

3 October 2017

In natural history it is easy to announce a first for the year, but to be mindful of the last is more difficult. I know now that the house martins are gone, yet their going from our village entailed an unremarkable dwindling of sights and sounds, but slowly like the loss of moisture from a puddle.

Last week I did have one memorable sighting of the bird in the Yare Valley. Over Blackwater about forty were pooled above a poplar plantation and in and out of their midst swirled a single lost swift. The martins were smaller, busier, each one with a swept-back wing silhouette which, depending on the way it turned, was shaped like a broad smile, or a frown.

They were feeding in a manner that entailed much even soaring, then passages of wing beats of about fifteen flickering strokes in bursts of 1–3 seconds. In those moments of intensity the birds would steeple higher, catch their fly, and then fall away, resuming the steady-state evenness of the glide. I estimated about forty, but only a dozen birds were visible at any moment and the rest were implied by an elastic net of dry buzzing notes that are the perpetual atmosphere in which house martins pass their lives.

It seemed to me that it was the outriders who vocalised most, reassuring themselves of contact with the rest, but providing a loose mobile web of calls with which all could keep company. And this sound, as simple as dried grass and as modest as insect stridulation, is the thing they take with them to Africa, and which I shall miss most.

Since this bird eats only invertebrates it is a call made of insects, but it is also much more. For house martins eat prey known as aerial plankton and the birds return to Europe only when these insects achieve a critical mass in the air above our land. But for now, as the light diminishes, as the warmth fades and as our hemisphere turns at an angle of 23.4 degrees away from the sun, so the insects disappear and thus the calls go south. Think, then, of the house martins' warm buzzy envelope of dry notes as the music of our planet turning in outer space.

## 4 October 2016

### ⤞ VIKOS GORGE, GREECE ⤝

This extraordinary Epirote valley is claimed to be the world's deepest gorge, and from a spot called Beloi it seemed a reasonable notion. Yet it must be said that reason is the part of the human faculties least appropriate to this experience. For, just to get there, you have to descend through a scramble of boulders and use all four limbs in tandem to map the next small awkward advance; until finally, at the canyon rim, where a chest-high wall encloses a small soil-floored cup with standing room for five, you look out, and it hits you.

How bizarre, you reflect later, that, poised on the edge of all this nothing – the guard wall balanced above a chasm of 700 metres – and with only the exquisite liquid quality of Greek light between you and mountains perhaps 20 kilometres away, you have suddenly felt lost for air.

In fact it was amusing to observe, as other pilgrims arrived, how the same inarticulate breathlessness could translate into so many different languages.

Earlier visitors had scratched their initials into the wall's smoothed surfaces and I tried to imagine them all, and all those languages, failing in this same sublime moment. That line of thought led me back to conjure a time when the first humans, clad in who knows what skins, clambered out here too and saw this place, and what strange and unrecorded words could they not find?

Then a wood warbler darted out and flitted across the edge of all this vast drama, and it forced me to reflect on an even greater tale. It was a migrant bird – in Vikos today, but tomorrow, perhaps, on Corfu and onwards, step by step, to the Congo. Then the swallows, which, gliding down this unspeakable abyss as if it were just one more sweet riff of air, may have bred in Poland or Ukraine but spend their winters in Durban. Wrapped right around our planet from Alaska to Vladivostok, it goes on: in our Claxton garden, in any quiet scrub pocket near where city commuters walk to work, but also here at Vikos. Among the pedestrian and the sublime, these migrant birds are draining south among us all.

## 13 October 2007

### ⤙ Claxton, Norfolk ⤚

Showman, humorist, puppeteer, journalist, author, naturalist, illustrator, cartoonist and social historian. Most of us would agree that this roster of achievement by Arthur Patterson wouldn't be a bad innings for anyone. But for a man born into acute poverty it is remarkable. His precise birthday was 19 October 1857 and just in case the maths has momentarily eluded you, it means he was born exactly 150 years ago next Friday.

If you take the achievements all together he is one of the most gifted sons of his native Yarmouth in the borough's long history. By themselves they would ensure that he was worthy of remembrance. My own personal reason for noting Patterson's anniversary is to celebrate someone whom I consider among the most distinguished interpreters of the East Anglian landscape. In his books, Patterson provided a record of its historical character and of its distinctive human communities that was every bit as rich and important as the watercolours of John Sell Cotman or the photographs of P. H. Emerson.

The only Norfolk naturalist to compare with Patterson for sheer range of expertise and volume of output is Ted Ellis who, in fact, learnt some of his trade at Patterson's side. Not even Ellis, however, matches Patterson for the historical significance of his writings or the quality of the prose.

The other striking characteristic of Patterson's work is its localism. His mark is deeper for being narrower. His principal territory was the estuarine flatland at the Yare–Waveney confluence just downstream from where I live, known as Breydon Water. (It is, in fact, just across the valley from my favourite rookeries.) By focusing attention so completely on these marshes, the largest in lowland England, Patterson left a record which matches Gilbert White's for its intimacy and minuteness of detail.

Nationally he is almost unknown, yet he remains familiar and popular in his home county. A few of a particularly scarce vintage might even recall him as a writer in the pages of this newspaper [*Eastern Daily Press*], where he maintained various columns until his death in 1935. Most of his articles appeared under two striking noms de plume. As a naturalist he was the self-effacing 'John Knowlittle', a meticulous chronicler of Norfolk wildlife; as a humorist and keeper of the local dialect, Patterson donned a separate disguise – that of 'Melinda Twaddle', a feisty feminine source of home-grown wit and philosophy.

Anyone specifically interested in books about Norfolk will surely have encountered the man. In a career spanning nearly half a century he produced twenty-six works. None is still in print, although his great-granddaughter Beryl Tooley recently produced a selection of his words in *Scribblings of a Yarmouth Naturalist*. In second-hand bookshops original 'Pattersons' are usually in the glass cabinet with the other first editions, where they are highly prized and priced.

I must confess that my own love affair with his work was slow to mature and started on a false note. Many of the key works are studies of wildlife and the natural scene and, on first acquaintance, involve a rather narrow vocabulary on a single theme, such as *Notes of an East Coast Naturalist* (1904), *Nature in Eastern Norfolk* (1905), *Wildlife on a Norfolk Estuary* (1907), *Man and Nature on Tidal Waters* (1909). All of these were published by Methuen and there is a good deal of repetition from one to the other.

From all accounts the prose (as well as occasional poems and an inventive stream of humorous sketches and postcards) flowed from Patterson's pen with an easy and generous informality. Throughout his life he must have produced many millions of words. To use a rather exalted comparison, the poet T. S. Eliot once wrote of his contemporary D. H. Lawrence that he had to write much to write well. The same might be said of Patterson.

I would single out two books as most representative of his genius and the very best of a huge output. They are *Man and Nature on Tidal Waters* and a later book, which he dictated for typing to the young Ted Ellis, entitled *Wildfowlers and Poachers* (1929). It is notable that Patterson embarked on this second work three times over twenty years, costing him more effort than any of his other books and serving, in a sense, as a final digest of his reflections.

What distinguishes the best of Patterson is a remarkable ear for local dialect. In fact, his books are probably the single most important source on Norfolk speech patterns at the end of the nineteenth century. Not only could he hear and render it intelligible for non-natives (such as myself!), Patterson had a fabulous facility for recreating conversation. He caught not just the vocabulary, he conveyed the living music and pressing content of this distinctive patois as it flowed in real time. The thing that gave him such a ready access to the language was his lifelong friendship with the marshmen who dwelt around Breydon.

Looking back from a different millennium I find it hard to believe that such a community of Britons had ever existed so close to our own time. They were known locally as punt-gunners because of their weapon of choice – a huge-barrelled fowling piece that could discharge half a pound of lead in a single shot and down scores, if not, on rare occasions, hundreds of shore birds. The punt-gunners were no less hunter-gatherers than the Boran of East Africa or the Yanomami of the South American rainforest.

Their entire livelihoods, almost everything they owned, traded or consumed, except their copious quantities of pipe tobacco, came from the local environment. They were brilliant trackers of game and expert anglers. Even a simple list of their names conveys something of their tough character and distinctive appearance – figures like Short'un Page, Pintail Thomas, Salt-fish Jex, Limpenny Joe, 'Silky' Watson and 'Cadger' Brown. They sound just like characters from a Dickens novel, and I am not the first to suggest that Patterson evoked their society with a typically Dickensian brilliance and warmth of tone.

Their favourite watering hole was an ancient establishment called the Bowling Green – alas no longer with us – that stood on the edge of Breydon estuary. 'There was a club-like air about the place,' Patterson wrote in *Wildfowlers and Poachers*, 'where men of kindred occupations and tastes could discuss over mugs and pewters their mutual rivalries and reminiscences.' In this strange context of barrels and bottles, bird skins and mounted fish, of sawdust-covered floors and spittoons and a pervasive, pungent cumulonimbus of pipe smoke, the author found a vanishing world.

'The lounging smokers on the worn settles,' he continued, some arguing guns and prowess with rough unmusical voices; others as silent and meditative, yet alert to pick up advantageous gossip, with lips focused into pouting rings, like touched sea anemones, into which short clay pipes had been thrust. The faces of the men, lined and hardened by storm and sun, were full of character, indexing a sturdy, contentious self-reliance.

Note that wonderfully visual and ecologically apt simile – their mouths pouted like 'touched sea anemones' – for these salt-crusted figures.

It is a fishing expedition undertaken by one of these hardy souls which forms the subject of another favourite and classic passage by Patterson. In *Man and Nature on Tidal Waters* he gives an account of eel-fishing across the fields beyond Breydon with a man called Tom Brookes. The number of separate traditional methods – babbing, flying, lamb-netting and lining, to name but a few – by which these marshmen could lure eels from their muddy domain probably exceeds the eel total in the whole of Breydon today. Yet in Patterson's time the fish were ten a penny or, as he specifies through Brookes and others, about nine pence a pound. During the course of the expedition, Patterson and Brookes spot a farmer coming towards them across the fields.

> Now Brookes had no desire that he [the farmer] should know we were doing fairly well, or the young man himself might bring into use his own lambing-net and so spoil future 'workings' in the neighbourhood. So while the young farmer was yet a long way off, Brookes deftly shot about seven pounds of eels from my sack into one he carried in his pocket, and pushed up his waistcoat! In my own bag there remained only three or four pounds of eels, which certainly did not appear to the new-comer an extraordinary catch when he peered into its depths and laughed at our labours. Brookes was by no means comfortable with his tightly-buttoned coat imprisoning the unhappy fishes; but our visitor, wishing us good luck, soon strode off on his round of cattle-watching.

In one short apparently simple paragraph Patterson captures, like an acutely observant anthropologist, the tricks of the trade, the unspoken rivalries and the individualist psychology of his tribal community, not to mention the visual comedy of one man engaging in apparently normal conversation and all the while deceiving his interlocutor with half a stone of eels shoved up his jumper.

In the course of one chapter, a mere dozen pages, Patterson evokes not just an afternoon of pleasant and productive sport, he gives us a detailed explication of lamb-netting as a technique, the natural ecology of the eel as a fish, he recounts record catches (32 pounds on one night), or rare nocturnal escapades involving a cow that hooked by accident a basket of the creatures on its horn, or memorable nuggets that entailed a pike with a water vole removed intact from its gut. More than this, Patterson conveys one whole form of subsistence livelihood that has now vanished from our regional countryside for ever.

I said at the beginning that Patterson is one of the most distinguished writers on nature in Norfolk, but it is this theme in particular – let us call it the human ecology of the Breydon marshmen – that I find so special. Conventional works of natural history would have given us the status, distribution and habits of the birds, fishes or other wildlife of east Norfolk. Patterson did all that. Yet he also added to the mix their numerous and complex interactions with the local humans. The end result is the most detailed portrait of any region of Norfolk – embracing people and place, the human and the natural, the cultural and its ecological context – from the late Victorian to the early Georgian period.

The impulse to locate ourselves at the heart of nature writing is now part of the mainstream of its modern form. Indeed his pioneering use of the trope makes Patterson seem acutely contemporary. Yet in *his* day it must have taken great courage to suggest that the Breydon tribe of fisherfolk and punt-gunners was worthy of serious literary attention. Remember that these were often the poorest of the rural poor, men and women who thought nothing of sitting down to roast gull or boiled dunlin for their supper. Many of them ended up penniless wards of the workhouses, yet Patterson showed us what a remarkable community lay beneath the salty grime or, as he himself called it, 'the ooze'.

There is one final dimension to Patterson's achievement that I referred to at the very beginning of my essay. He was able to get under the skin of working people because he shared their background lifestyle and origins. Born into extreme hardship in the insanitary, cramped 'Rows' of Yarmouth, Arthur Patterson was part of a family of seven children, only one of whom – Arthur himself – survived beyond twenty-one years of age.

Although he always looked dapper and distinguished with his pointed goatee – I think he often looks like a cross between Ezra Pound and W. H. Hudson – and was possibly the most photographed man in Great Yarmouth in his day, he was never really in good health and money was tight, particularly since he also had a family of seven children to support. His life assumed a steadier course when he acquired the most enduring of his jobs, that of Yarmouth's 'kiddy-catcher' or truant officer, but he frequently lamented how straitened circumstances and his lowly status curtailed his achievements.

A typical example of how conventional Georgian society contrived to diminish Patterson's work concerned his relations with the Linnean Society. The London-based natural science institution received proposals for Patterson's elevation to associate member as early as 1906. They deigned to bestow it upon him in 1935, just months before he died.

Another snub closer to home came when he worked tirelessly to create a museum in Great Yarmouth and helped to secure most of its natural historical exhibits. At the inaugural address a man called F. Danby Palmer, the chair of the launch committee of which Patterson was secretary, gave a speech highlighting his own glorious achievements as sole creator of the museum. At the mayor's 'at home' party Patterson was ignored by the servants, who didn't even offer him so much as a cup of tea. All we can say, by way of making small amends, is to wonder who will celebrate the 150th anniversary of F. Danby Palmer.

It is not just a case of Arthur Patterson's achievements being especially impressive despite his background poverty. It is that poverty itself made his achievements possible in the first place. Without having experienced the same social and cultural circumstances of many of his Yarmouth contemporaries, in his writing Patterson could never have got so close to the truth of his times. This Friday I shall raise a champagne toast to his hardships, and celebrate the life of this wonderfully multi-talented son of the local soil. I hope you'll join me.

## 13 October 2013

### LLANYSTUMDWY, GWYNEDD

The water of the Dwyfor is turned black as the sun falls and as the falling shadows of the wood thicken on either riverbank. Black, but for the surf rinse that washes round every boulder in its course and then the stepped white sheets folding over where the weir takes the current down, then down again.

Upstream the beeches are still loaded with green over the place where David Lloyd George is buried. Earlier in the day, that very same spot was loud with the workman trill of wrens as they hammered and drilled those invincible phrases into the enfolded gloom. Yet now it is all quiet, but for the river's gush. In fact, the whole place has an aura of things under the power of gravity. Not just the trail of leaves down from the canopy, nor the eddy of other leaves from upstream that are carried in swirls at the river's margin; it's everything – the cold air, the falling current, the failing light, the mood of the entire place – they're all coming down.

And where it all whooshes under the bridge in that controlled torrent of air and water, I can see a dipper mid-stream on its boulder perch. Lack of light reduces this pied bird merely to the tiny planet of white stretched across its breast. Dippers are creatures of immense character but this is nothing but a pale blob in the gloom.

As I observe more closely through the binoculars, it sweeps a beak to preen flanks free of loose river droplets, and the whiteness morphs, twisting with the effort or expanding in relaxation. Then the beak opens and out of it (I infer; since I cannot actually hear it) comes all that strange rambling sweetness of dipper song. I do not hear it because it too is all carried downstream in the relentless seaward thrum of the Dwyfor. Yet this rotund bird, river-sculpted like a pebble itself, indifferent to the autumn and the current and that figure on the bridge, sings on.

## 14 October 2014

### ⤚ BLACKWATER CARR, NORFOLK ⤙

They burst from the trees and the mixture of clattered vegetation and the sound of stiff fletch upon the air revealed them instantly as wood pigeons. The species is so abundant these days that in the minds of many naturalists it now occupies a form of negative space. They look at them primarily to dismiss them. Yet the occasional singleton at least requires you to notice the diagnostic white half-collar on the neck, or that curving band of white across the short wing, or even just the flat, even, hammering of its broad beat to reassure yourself of its identity; that it is merely the commonplace creature you assumed and not something more engaging, like a sparrowhawk or a lone stock dove.

Yet our indifference overlooks the wonderful contributions made by wood pigeons. I love the coarse throaty song, with its characteristic five-note motif, that's so much the background music to British woods. I love too those strange mock battles performed by males, when they strike each other with open wings and fill the treetops with the noise of their hollow bluster. I love most of all those moments in midwinter when they can seem sublimely beautiful – the flock coming down on to a field and the broken silver arc of their underwings turned purer than white by reflected snow.

These experiences should force us at least to recall that the
wood pigeon cannot be blamed for the darker symbolism it has
recently acquired. Since the 1960s the population has increased
by 170 per cent. The species' catholicity in food and habitat, as
well as its wider adaptations to humans, means that it thrives in
our massively simplified countryside, where so many others birds
now fail. Wood pigeons go on increasing and while we may not
notice their abundance, visiting friends from Africa or Spain are
alert to a countryside which, to them, seems full of nothing but
wood pigeons. It has become less an expression of abundance as
an emblem of loss. Today pigeons represent a biomass not much
less than that of all the other songbirds in Britain.


17 October 2017

⤜ CRESSBROOK DALE, DERBYSHIRE ⤛

I find it strange to read in Oliver Rackham's wonderful *Trees
and Woodland in the British Landscape* that sycamores were probably
introduced to the UK in the sixteenth century, but only went
native in the eighteenth. It seems odd, because it is hard to imagine
this restless beast of a tree settling for domestic imprisonment
for 200 years.

My experience is that its whirling helicopter-like 'keys',
aided only by the slightest breeze, can unpick any attempt to
block their escape into the wild. In our Norfolk village I am also
astonished how quickly those seeds put down roots and I've even
taken to using mole grips to wrestle with the saplings' iron-like
purchase on our garden soil.

Yet as you travel around the Peak District National Park,
especially in a triangle defined by the towns of Buxton, Ashford
and Hartington, sycamores have a more benign presence. Look
across those folded plains of limestone-walled pasture and it's
often the only tree species visible. In this landscape sycamores
create clumps of deep colour and shade that have something of

the monumental quality present in Paul Nash's paintings of his beloved elms.

On a recent walk during an October downpour I also discovered another act of kindness by this often despised 'foreigner'. The broad palms of the sycamore's hand-like leaves make the canopy a natural umbrella. At this season they may not produce the same intense colour of late beech or horse chestnut, but sycamores certainly add to the sense of slow-smoking afterglow, which is such a glorious part of the Derbyshire woods in autumn rain.

They also make other major contributions to the atmosphere in and around the Wye Valley. In Chee Dale, for instance, sycamores are often entirely smothered to their twig ends in an overcoat of almost fluorescent moss, so that they generate an aura of ongoing life even in midwinter. Here in Cressbrook Dale they were thickly clothed in moss and ivy and then wreathed with epiphytic polypody ferns. For now no rook-delighting heaven could find any route into this sub-canopy scene and that enclosed world of infinite greens had the monochrome mood and character of temperate rainforest.


## 18 October 2016

### CLAXTON, NORFOLK

Even in death it looked perfect, spots on his chest as bold as a summer's morning. It was a dead song thrush. The tiny yellow tips to the coverts and the faintest crease of like colour at the corners of the beak suggested a bird of the year, inexperienced in the ways of cats or windows. Yet what to do with something so beautiful?

First I had work. Our garden is split in three – vegetables down one side, a middle lawn running all the way to autumn's only colour, a cyclamen patch in the shadows under the hollies, and on the other side, by the hedge, for the last eight years, it has been left entirely to steer its own course. This third is now rank and flowerless and in need of cutting, but at midsummer there were fifteen wild flower species. I am at a loss to explain why so much meadow has been colonised by marjoram. It self-seeded from a cultivated sprig elsewhere but has come to occupy one whole section of the garden, even launching more satellite colonies to the lawn's middle.

As the scythe blade gathered in all those brittle stems there were one or two surprises: a lost beer bottle tossed in from a summer party and the scalp of a yellow meadow ants' nest, whose owners, mercifully, had vanished underground. What was shocking was the thick powerful odour of the herb, a smell that somehow has to come right into the nose and throat before being lodged fully, as if its dense oily qualities need air and moisture to flourish. Mixing something of the kitchen and of the hospital, this great rising balloon of last summer's breath permeated everywhere. Before settling down into the cleaner, simpler, sweet smell of cut grass and soil, it brought to mind its heyday: hoverflies in hundreds circulating that herb patch in a perpetual scatter dance of yellow and magenta.

I laid my song thrush down in the earth where all those life scenes and memories and scents arose. On the garden table the beer bottle stood as a totem of its only season. The cyclamens looked like lit tapers in the gloom.

## 19 October 2013

### ❧ REEPHAM, NORFOLK ❧

As we walked along the track, the dregs of a heavy downpour and the last light of day were both screened by the leaf lattice in the ash trees overhead. Along with cameras and binoculars we were both carrying an unusual item for a wildlife outing – a picnic chair apiece. But then this wasn't my usual nature excursion.

I was with the author and journalist Patrick Barkham and we were hoping to find an animal that has been his obsession for the last few years. The chairs reflected the fact that we were after a creature demanding stillness, silence, luck and a good deal of patience from the would-be observer. Even now the beast is still tricky to find locally. Proof of this is the fact that in thirty years I've never actually seen a live one in Norfolk.

When I was young, however, badgers seemed more myth than resident of the Derbyshire countryside. I was nineteen before I even glimpsed one dart across a Staffordshire road late at night. All of these developments – the gradual shift in its population, the badger's iconic place in the British imagination and the agricultural controversy that now centres on its official slaughter – are richly covered in Barkham's new book *Badgerlands*, which was released this month.

The author has more reason than most to be engaged with the fate of badgers. His maternal grandmother Jane Ratcliffe was passionately committed to the rehabilitation of injured animals, but when she took charge of an endearing bundle called 'Bodger', she also began to take up the badger's cause politically. Through the channels of the Women's Institute, Ratcliffe campaigned to have the animal legally protected.

In the mid-twentieth century, despite the nation's growing environmental awareness, the baiting of badgers and other forms of brutal 'sport' were still widely practised. Partly because of pressure from the WI, a pioneering piece of legislation was passed in 1973 to outlaw the digging out of setts and recreational slaughter of badgers.

In many ways the law was innovative but overdue. For the British had had a love affair with badgers for most of the century, partly because of the success of Kenneth Grahame's *The Wind in the Willows*. Barkham skilfully examines the impact of writers like Grahame but also others such as Henry Williamson and the great badger expert Ernest Neal. He shows how these more positive portrayals cemented a new image of the creature in the national consciousness. Badgers of the nineteenth century and earlier had been violent, curmudgeonly savages that warranted persecution or hunting with dogs. In Grahame's gentle classic, however, the badger morphed into an honest and moral citizen of the British countryside with ancient title deeds to his woodland residence.

Part of the joy of Barkham's book is the way he moves between these wider literary and cultural considerations to more lyrical evocations of place and moment. He has a poet's eye for natural detail. Coming upon a badger's sett amid a carpet of flowering bluebells, he suggests how 'two sandy spoil heaps from the tunnelling were as bright as coral cays in this blue sea'. The luxuriant blooms of rhododendrons seem as if they were 'plumped up like pillows in the garden'.

However Barkham's sophisticated grasp of the controversial linkage between badgers and bovine TB is the main reason that *Badgerlands* deserves to be a key text to inform this polarised debate. He treads a delicate line between his naturalist's sympathy for a glorious animal and a clear understanding of the economic and agricultural anxieties faced by farmers whose dairy herds are ravaged by this disease.

Barkham listens intently to both sides but challenges the idea that we can always sacrifice the lives of our fellow creatures for our own personal interest. His concluding arguments draw heavily upon a journal paper by a group of professional veterinarians who argued that TB, whether in cattle or humans, is a condition of poverty. There are the straitened conditions suffered by struggling managers of livestock herds, but there is also the genetic poverty of the cattle themselves.

The animals that form our dairy herds have been selectively bred and reared, invariably using artificial insemination, and drawing only upon breeds with high milk yields. The end result of this agricultural regime is cattle without a broad-based genetic heritage that can evolve natural resistance to TB. The issue of badgers and bovine TB asks that we question not just the methods of agricultural marksmen, or the short-term politics of

Westminster, but also the simplified economics implicit in our society's whole approach to food production.

Meanwhile our badger excursion looked as if it was fizzling out in exactly the way of many previous forays – towards absolute failure. Then suddenly, breaking the nocturnal cold and stillness, Patrick leant forward from his chair and pointed down the slope into the gloom. I peered intently and there it was, like a moving slurry of leaf-litter and earth with three stripes of moonlight running through its dark snout. It truffled down the bank and merged again with the shadows. It was a badger, my first Norfolk badger. In that moment the cold of night was displaced by a warm glow of pleasure.

## 20 October 2015

### ✖ CLAXTON, NORFOLK ✖

As I sat reading in the garden I could hear what I thought was the rustle of a tiny animal in the near hedge. Each time I turned round to see there was no visual cue or clearer sound to locate its author. That puzzle continued for a couple of minutes until the penny finally dropped: the noise was coming from on top of my head. So I painstakingly lifted the peak and lowered my cap until, sure enough, there was a common darter dragonfly blithely sunning itself still in my cradled hands. I could now appreciate how the faint rubbing of those plasticised wings was the source of its intermittent message. As we observed one another I wondered what its vast compound eyes, heritage of the Carboniferous, made of its admirer.

I doubt there was any sentiment on the part of one of us, but at least I was moved. Why are these moments of connection with other wild creatures so special? Yet they are truly. On his Facebook and Twitter page a friend still commemorates the moment a lime hawkmoth perched on his nose. Henry Thoreau had a sparrow once land on his shoulder and 'felt that I was more distinguished by that circumstance than I should have been by any epaulet I could have worn'.

The best such story I've heard this year was one by John Lister-Kaye of his friend Gavin Maxwell. The former had found a snared fox with its leg grotesquely cheese-wired by an illegal snare. Despite his best efforts he couldn't free the snarling human-hating beast and went to Maxwell, who instantly leapt in the boat to go to the rescue. When they approached the wounded animal there ensued the same painful routine of struggling interspecific bitterness. But gradually Maxwell, talking, reassuring all the while, got closer and closer. As he spoke so he soothed the fox's temper until eventually trust blossomed and Maxwell painstakingly prised open the wire trap and freed his fox. Maxwell's private and personal life was a train wreck but with this tale he had never seemed more admirable and human. It's not just that we join the other animals in these moments: it is that we lose that human heritage, as old as a sharpened stick, that we all must own.

28 October 2013

⤙ᘒ CLAXTON, NORFOLK ᘒ⤚

It is strange that sometimes it is the smallest things that reveal the largest themes. Despite the sun and warm still air in our lanes I felt mildly oppressed by the silence of this autumn morning. Then I stopped to watch the insects on the ivy. All along the hedge I could hear the indeterminate and random susurration of foliage interacting with the leg and body movements of the wasps, bluebottles and ichneumons that swarmed upon it. Then there was the delicious quiet snick of red admiral wings as it looped back and forth before settling on those lime-green flowers to probe for nectar.

It gradually dawned that there was a sparse autumn music; one needed simply to adjust to its subtle register. Here came a tit flock whose call-and-answer routine wrapped their unhurried movements in buoyant chat. Other flakes of sound came clean out of the blue from birds passing overhead. There was the flat downward seepage of meadow pipit notes along with the brighter calls of chaffinches, which you know are only grains from a larger harvest as Europe-wide now immense migrant flocks pass south and west.

There was even a kind of soundscape of my own creation. The robin, for instance, was tacking nervously now but earlier it had infused the whole lane with its song. Words are so ill-fitted to capture this fey music, although it seems to possess an indefinably twisting quality as if the entire drift of autumn colours were being lightly spun and then entwined in all that air and sunlight as a recurrent thread of melancholy. There were also the convulsive stupid sounds of young pheasants – a hoarse *kekking* complaint as they flew – and finally a cluster of jackdaws looping over the church when I opened the gate. A cloak of *jak-jak-jakking* accompanied its going. Yet these birds were neither angry nor anxious, they merely carried off with them that atmosphere of conviviality that always seems the prerequisite of jackdaw lives.

### 28 October 2014

### BERGH APTON, NORFOLK

The difference between a fungus foray and most other forms of nature study is the sheer gregariousness of it all. There were more than twenty of us, aged eight to eighty, joking and laughing and clustered around our guide, who was himself like a rare treasured specimen. Tony Leech is an expert who contributes as much simple human joy to a group as he does forensic knowledge.

Equally these mushroom outings are as participatory as they are communal. Each person scoured the ground for his or her own contribution and brought it to the central hub of discussion. Our guide, in turn, marshalled these converging tributaries of enquiry into a wider delta of mycological conversation. This one was a dryad saddle. There was a wood blewit, or parrot waxcap, a collared earthstar. I often stood simply to marvel at the sheer poetry of mushroom nomenclature. Just ponder awhile the wrinkled peach, the parasol, the lilac bonnet but also the dog stinkhorn.

It was also an excursion involving all the senses. We lay on the ground to be on intimate terms with the tiny earthtongue or dead moll's fingers, whose pencil-thin fruiting bodies poked up like blackened digits. We inhaled a deep whiff of ocean in a mushroom called crab brittlegill. Best of all, we stood in sheer amazement at the crazy fecundity of fungi: a single fruit body of the football-sized giant puffball can produce six billion spores.

Eventually the whole afternoon of encounter between humans and fungi was distilled to Tony Leech's basket of specimens. Here were gathered all the toadstools that were beyond our collective ken, and whose identities can sometimes only be settled by examination of spores that are $1/200^{th}$ of a millimetre. In a sense that collection symbolised all that our own species has pondered, learnt and felt about mushrooms for centuries. Yet that same basket also summarised the unfathomable wonder of life on this planet: for it contained the stories of 100 different fungi, which have each travelled through time probably for millions of years to meet on that afternoon in that October sunshine.

# NOVEMBER

## 1 November 2016

### ◆◈ CLAXTON, NORFOLK ◈◆

I was amused recently by my neighbour who described her love affair with a robin called 'Robbie' – a decade-long passion that is probably three times the average lifespan of a robin. Since both sexes of the bird sing and cannot always tell each other's genders, my neighbour may actually have loved many 'Robbies' over the years. Yet no matter! Her love is true.

It is interesting to compare my neighbour's engagement with nature to the public responses at Lough Beg in County Derry, Northern Ireland, which I visited recently. Lough Beg is part of 'Seamus Heaney Country', the landscape central to the Nobel Laureate's magnificent poetry. A proposed four-lane highway would violate Heaney's heartland and wildlife areas protected by numerous international designations. Yet in the absence of protest from more mainstream NGOs (the RSPB and Ulster Wildlife Trust), a friend is fighting a lone legal battle, supported by his own money and crowd sourcing.

On Kent's Hoo Peninsula, meanwhile, there is a contest to save Lodge Hill, a woodland that is home to about ninety nightingale pairs, as well as an host of other wildlife that justifies its statutory protection as an SSSI. Yet the MOD wants to build 5,000 homes there. More parochially the University of East Anglia in Norfolk wants to site a 300-vehicle car park on the last really important habitat at the heart of Norwich.

What these stories reflect is a situation painstakingly described in two *State of Nature* reports published in 2013 and 2016. The documents catalogue how nature is undergoing systemic decline in our country. In the three cases named the supporters of development – including all the political parties in Northern Ireland, the MOD in Kent and the university authorities here – seem to see nature as an abstract idea, a theoretical resource, which can withstand any amount of imposition.

Somehow they fail to see that nature is, in truth, that marsh, that wood, this particular field and even this individual bird. They could all learn much from my neighbour, who sees nature as the robin singing directly to her. What she values is the lived encounter. For the robin as idea is a trifle that can so easily be turned from vague abstraction into mere memory.

### 3 November 2015

### ⊱ CLAXTON, NORFOLK ⊰

One of the striking aspects of starling flocks is the lack of rhythm in their flight. They look all metropolitan bustle and hurry but as I emerge on the track by the marsh I can hear the air rush through all those wings. Then there comes that eternal rash of brittle notes that is the essence of starling palaver. It forms the audible atmosphere in which all such flocks dwell.

There are about 400 birds, probably fresh in on yesterday's north-easterlies and originally from Russia or perhaps Poland. Yet it is odd to think of them as chimney-pot solitaries in Warsaw or Krakow – where they call them 'szpak' – each producing that quirky wing-flicking spring bluster, or stabbing worm mush into the yellow-lined flowerhead mouths of their begging youngsters.

Here, now they all behave as a single organism and it comes towards me along the edge of the dyke. It rolls forward in clusters of ten or twenty. Each sub-flock plumps down and vanishes in turn. Others come on behind, relentlessly. And in this way it arrives before me as a tumbleweed of moving birds. Occasionally two of them, newly vanished, suddenly pop back up, all legs and squabbling beaks, then they fall apart and resume the stab-and-prise feeding technique that scientists call *Zirkeln*.

Routinely something in the mood of our marsh catches these eastern newcomers unawares and up they blizzard. The flock hurtles forward then drops into neutral, every wing beat ceasing briefly, and it stall-glides back to Earth before a final flurry of effort as they settle once more as a dark moving stain. Rarest of all is the moment that several birds perch on a five-bar gate where I can scrutinise them in detail, the young and adults, the males and females. I can admire their emerald iridescence, the violaceous gloss and the newly moulted spotting, which looks somewhere between hail on freshly set tar and stars in the night.

When they go again I sense they will not stop this time. They become mere smudges of darkness far off against the distant willows and soon they are sheeting into someone else's field. Mine is all empty and quiet, but for the dour notes of rooks and the sitting gulls, all autumnal and morose.


## 7 November 2017

### ⤚ ROCKLAND ST MARY, NORFOLK ⤙

There were two catchers of fish at the water's edge. There was the old boy who told me he had been coming here for fifty years and then there was the grey heron that has acquired a deep familiarity with people. I often see it as I drive through the neighbouring village of Bramerton, where it stands by the pond right at the roadside.

Today it was on Rockland staithe, where it kept a companionable distance from its human neighbour. Both faced towards the tide-swollen water and while both were fish-focused only one was doing the catching. He told me that the heron has been a regular at the spot for about ten years and over that time has acquired the courage to pace within touching distance of his pitch. On winter mornings when the ground is frozen and pickings are slim, the bird stands on an adjacent telegraph pole and croaks his disapproval. Apparently the fishermen have taken this as a sign of its hunger and they toss it parts of their unwanted catch.

As if on cue, the line tightened while we spoke and out from the staithe rose a fish – a small perch – sudden and otherworldly and sparkling even in this November grey. What followed seemed all highly rehearsed. The man disconnected the fish from the hook. The heron stalked straight at him. The man made a gesture as if to throw and the very moment the fish hit the ground, down stabbed the beak. I had time just to register the oxygen-rich red pulsing in a semicircle at the gills and then there was that strange convulsion of neck muscles as the bird and fish combined; and then all was over.

As the heron gazed out I noticed how the long plumes, brushed slightly by the breeze, were flexed and twisted at its neck, like the silver willow leaves falling all around. The beak had something of the orange-yellow of horse chestnut leaves and its neck feathers had the faintest blush of the wine-stain colour now present in guelder rose and it struck me that this somnolent well-fed bird seemed the very essence of this autumn scene.

## 11 November 2013

### ⤖ BLACKWATER CARR, NORFOLK ⤖

If ever a spider could soften the knee-jerk reactions of the average arachnophobe, then I suspect it would be the marbled orb-weaver. The one I stumbled across was about as captivating as they get. The whole of its body was a rich, almost edible, buttery yellow that resembled that glorious sun-coloured inner corolla to a primrose flower.

Yet this only half captures the full appeal of this particular species, because across the hind part of its abdomen, the marbled orb-weaver possesses a leaf-like pattern of contrasting shade. In many it is a deep mahogany brown, but on this female it was the exact tone of an old oak leaf caught in winter sunlight. It also had a fretted quality like a window shutter carved out in ornate Arabic calligraphy. In truth the whole beast conjured for me something decidedly Islamic. As well as the primrose and the oak, its colours evoked nothing so much as those fabulous silk-soft babouche slippers that are arranged in exquisite rows to tempt passers-by in the labyrinthine markets of Marrakesh or Fez.

The skein of connections unravelling from those colours was only one part of this spider's associations. For, until I disturbed it and it scrambled away, the beast had clung true and squat amid the perfection of its own creation. From that place at the wheel's hub the radials of silk had run outwards at 12–15 degree intervals. Is it not moving to recall that spider webs are spun from a fabric that evolved more than 350 million years ago?

So when you encounter an orb-weaver web you are looking not only at the brief moment of this sphere, but also catching a glimpse of the Earth before even dinosaurs had walked it. If you then get down to the spider's eye level, you can appreciate how those glistening lines, which are just three-thousandths of a millimetre across, spread outwards to enmesh the sun, the light, the sky and the whole surrounding landscape.

## 15 November 2016

### ⋙ THE MAJOR OAK, NOTTINGHAMSHIRE ⋘

Although British place names make frequent reference to different tree species, there can be few road signs giving directions to a single specimen. Nor can there be many English woods more steeped in story than Sherwood Forest.

I found a few incidental tales even as I walked up to the tree. There were fairy bonnet mushrooms painting their way across a dead stump like Lowry crowds through Salford. There were some last wasps around a waste bin and wood pigeons so glutted on acorns their crops bulged like moneybags. A robin laced its sad song among the birches, but sadder still was a bench with the following inscribed across its seat: 'Abby Louise Hucknall – Missed So Much'. An emotional counterpoint came amid much open-armed laughter from the children playing along a Halloween-themed trail.

Then I arrived at the clearing and there was the biggest story of them all. It began about 1,100 years ago and has acquired a 10-metre waistband and two enormous stegosaurus-tail limbs, whose reach measures 90 metres around the top. The tree has worn out several names down the years – Cockpen Tree, Queen's Oak – and even its modern version derives from an eighteenth-century historian, Major Rooke.

In time we have mingled anxiety with awe and in 1908 slung steel harnesses and chains to cradle vulnerable branches. By 1975, along with our hands-on affections, came trampling feet that compacted the ground and starved the tree of nutrients. Now there are ten steel support buttresses and a high fence around to hold the estimated five million visitors every decade at an oak's arm's length from too much intimacy.

Yet why exactly should we privilege this one organism with all our reverence? After all, those fairy bonnets or the wasps are chemically more complex than any lifeless planet out in the galaxy. The wood pigeons rising out of the woodland bear aloft a heritage of flight dating back to the Jurassic. Or is it, perhaps, a simpler human-sized story: that after 400,000 days on Earth, this magnificent oak is still full of life, like those playing children, while much-missed Abby Hucknall, alas, is not?

17 November 2015

～ Claxton, Norfolk ～

On these exceptionally still days I go to the copse by the marsh to listen to its subtlety one more time. You have to work to pick it out behind the blackbird commotion or the jay screech: a snick as a stalk breaks free and the leaf lullabies down. Often there is also the patter of its zigzag tumble through the branches and then a quiet rustle once it settles among the trees' heap of old clothes. The summer woods are disrobing and you can hear them do so one leaf at a time.

It is apt that in India they eat food off leaves because leaves feed the whole planet. Ponder this Devonian miracle, if you will, and not just its 400-million-year-old architecture but also the fact that terrestrial plant life covers 75 per cent of the Earth's land surface. Each year it produces half the estimated 105 billion tonnes of photosynthesised biomass (the other half is the work of marine phytoplankton). And then each leaf blows out summer long the oxygen we need and sucks in the carbon breath we don't.

Even dead leaves give us what Victor Hugo defined as the usefulness of beauty. In a tree-lined park recently the cast foliage lay in separate stripes as if an artist had blown different coloured paint powders between the tree trunks. There were biscuit-toned poplar leaves, the tanned leather of the maples, the dying coals of fallen beech. Between these muted shades were two lines of ginkgo leaves. Also known as the maidenhair tree, it is a Chinese import and the last of its kind on Earth. Not a single ginkgo leaf was anything but unalloyed dull gold. The oak trees remained a fierce standing brazier of orange and the horse chestnuts were caught halfway. The dropped foliage formed a copper circle; the retained stuff was yellowing with the last green fingers on lower boughs.

There is a final pleasure to autumn woods in which we can play an active part. All the extravagant crunch comes from the leaves, but the rhythm of their music is shaped entirely by our own feet.

21 November 2017

⤙ HOLME, NORFOLK ⤚

It's funny how kingfishers, the boldest-coloured birds in Britain, have inspired so much confusion. The commonest example

concerns their size. Many people seeing one for the first time
are flabbergasted at its smallness. A recent encounter reminded
me just how sparrow-like they are. For twenty minutes I had
sat before a pool scanning the middle distance for harriers and
winter geese, before noticing a kingfisher had been perched there
all the time. It was only when it made its silvery piping notes that
I fixed its location on a reedmace head.

It then caught three sticklebacks and battered each on a
favourite perch, before gulping them down. This hearty appetite
chimes with another key fiction. Kingfishers were viewed as
remorseless destroyers of fish. While some of this is true – a
nesting pair can catch 115 fish in one day – almost all their prey
are minnows and sticklebacks. Unfortunately the owners of trout
fisheries thought otherwise and, according to David Bannerman,
'almost exterminated the bird in the nineteenth century'.

Even more mystifying was the proscribing of kingfishers
through the 1566 Acte for the Preservation of Grayne, which
also operated on the delusion that the dipper and kingfisher
were the same species. Bounties were paid for both and even
in 1879 the Duchess of Sutherland authorised the slaughter
of 368 dippers. Alas for that species: it mainly eats caddisfly
larvae.

However, the most enduring kingfisher myth owes its 2,000-
year history partly to Aristotle, the founder of Western science,
who claimed that the bird made its nest on the sea surface in
a period of winter calm. Incidentally, this is where we got the
phrase 'halcyon days', which are now – of course – synonymous
with summer.

The idea that kingfishers were associated with calm weather
meant that their feathers were kept as charms to ward off thunder
or for general good fortune. A naturalist travelling in Russia
noted that a distraught local blamed his wife's death on the loss
of his kingfisher amulet. Most of these untruths have had baleful
consequences for this bird of sky and flame, but there is one
myth I rather like: only the righteous get to see them.

## 25 November 2013

### ⤳ CLAXTON, NORFOLK ⤳

We know that at some level there's no such thing as a season or month or week or even a day. There is just the liquid passage of time flowing across our lives that we chop and segment with these invented names to give it all clarity and structure. Yet this morning truly seemed a moment loaded with symbolism. It felt like a hinge. It came with that first back sweep of the bedroom curtain and its revelation of a lawn silvered with something heavier than dew. Then I noticed that the wasps' nest, whose fortunes I've followed daily, was finally dormant. Dead leaves had already half-obliterated the mouse-sized hole from which workers had earlier flowed ceaselessly; but not now the frost has stung the ground into white silence.

Over the marsh there were other insignia of change. For the first time in ages a peregrine wound around a marsh harrier and buzzard in long loops, while all about these hard-edged predators was a softer chaff of rooks calling and fussing nervously. These raptors were suggestive of the new season but what came next was proof.

The sounds drifted first out of the wide blue to the east and mingled with the more usual calls of herring gulls. In fact it was some seconds before I started to differentiate the sweet wailing of one from the soft yodelling of the other. There were four wild swans, the adults fore and aft of their two grey-mottled offspring. Bewick's swans migrate to Norfolk from the 70th parallel north. The two youngsters – born this summer in some swathe of tundra with its coarse Russian winds and ceaseless Arctic light – were visiting these islands for the first time. Sandwiched between the adults and enfolded in the latter's quiet bell-like notes of reassurance, the immature birds sustained the exact same rhythmic beat of their parents' wings; yet one wondered if those young swan hearts were quickened by the startling vision of Norfolk's winter fields.

## 25 November 2014

### ~⊙ CLAXTON, NORFOLK ⊙~

Recently at my wood and across parts of our lawn I've been practising an al fresco number that involves a lot of heel grinding and foot stomping in methodical lines back and forth across the turf. However, this jig is only part of the full routine. Earlier I'd close-mown both patches, roughed it up badly with a rake, sprinkled the bare ground with round papery seeds and finally jumped all over it. If I had to give a name to the whole performance I'd call it the 'yellow rattle dance'.

Subtle and mischievous, yellow rattle is really the flower with everything. It was once found over millions of acres of British meadow and just a few of the old names – 'bull's pease', 'dog's pennies', 'money-grass', 'poverty-weed' and 'shacklebags' – give a sense of the cultural stories once entwined round its erect pubescent stem. The flower has strange laterally flattened yellow petals, complete with violet-coloured 'buck teeth' that emerge from their calyx like a puppet's head out of a box. But this species now combines beauty with purpose, for its best trick is to filch nutrients from the roots of neighbouring grasses and it's this parasitism that I hope to incorporate into our lawn's ecology.

I'm seeking the inverse of the standard engineered rye-grass monoculture. The yellow rattle dance is, in fact, the culmination of years of draining fertility from the lawn and by weakening the grass further, this wonderful plant creates space for native flowers with good nectar sources for insects. What a strange world we live in when the average crop field annually receives twenty chemical applications and the wider countryside has lost 99 per cent of its flower-rich meadows and when our gardens – amounting to just over one million acres – are the last potential resource for places rich in wild flowers. However, making mini-meadows of our gardens requires that we shuffle over a bit with the trampoline and barbie and let go a little on the lawnmower's throttle. I can only suggest that the butterflies, hoverflies, moths, grasshoppers and Buglife will all love you.

27 November 2014

CLAXTON, NORFOLK

In environmentalism as in modern politics, it seems the local and native are indisputably good, but the foreigner is viewed with suspicion. Take, for example, the mink, grey squirrel and signal crayfish, which are widely despised and blamed for their adverse effects on our own decent, upstanding indigenous wildlife. All three of the unpopular critters are originally American and were brought over and introduced by humans.

However, as in politics, so in environmentalism, there are exceptions that make life more complicated than some of us would wish. I'm thinking in particular of a wonderful 'foreign' creature, arguably the most endearing of our predatory birds, that is a favourite for farmers and naturalists alike. Yet technically this incomer still has minimal legal protection and is classified with other non-native animals.

It arrived in this country in the nineteenth century. Until then the English Channel had proved an insuperable barrier and, while people were said to keep it as a pet, primarily to eliminate invertebrate pests from the domestic interior, it had no genuine rights of residence. All this changed when a few landowners, particularly a Victorian ornithologist called Lord Lilford, released birds into the wild. On mild evenings in spring, the good folk of Northamptonshire or Kent were soon hearing the same soft, slightly melancholic piping note that I now delight to hear in the Yare Valley. Its owner is the small beast with a huge personality – the little owl.

Within seventy years it had spread across the English and Welsh countryside from Cornwall to the Scottish borders, but this colonisation was not without opposition. Gamekeepers routinely accused it of being harmful to young pheasants and partridges. Yet the research of a pioneer ecologist, Alice Hibbert-Ware, proved the shooting establishment almost entirely wrong. She showed that while little owls were something of a terror to crane flies and earwigs they were innocent of the game-killing accusations. Since that time little owls have come to be seen in a wholly positive light and have had no obvious adverse impact upon native species.

They are generalists par excellence, with a taste for large insects, but, on occasions, will take prey as large as wood pigeons or magpies. They are often valued by farmers and not just for their pest-clearance service, but because the birds have such bold, inquisitive personalities. Unlike other members of its family the little owl is often met by day. Looking like a white-spotted ball, the bird perches proprietorially on some high post or wire, bobbing its head, knitting together two striking white eyebrows to give it an air of quizzical irritation. The staring eyes take in any human intruder and on deciding that perhaps the two-legged creature below is just a little too large even for one as fierce as itself, the owl retreats in a distinctive bounding flight.

Alas, all of this wonderful owlish spirit is vanishing from our countryside. Something in the modern world – probably agricultural intensification – does not agree with little owls. They have declined by as much as 64 per cent since the 1960s and, although they might be loved by many they have not received the attention of other high-profile species, while their anomalous legal status has been a barrier to effective support.

However, the Norfolk-based Hawk and Owl Trust has helped to fund an important research project conducted by an ecologist every bit as dedicated as Alice Hibbert-Ware. Based at Reading University, Emily Joachim has made an exhaustive examination of the kinds of habitats little owls prefer, as well their movements and their choices of nest site. Smallholdings with open ground, short grass, livestock, undisturbed outbuildings, old orchards and even a touch of dereliction all feature strongly in the little owl's preferences.

Thirty years ago the Hawk and Owl Trust was at the forefront of efforts to reverse declines in another charismatic bird of East Anglia, the barn owl. Since their research in the mid 1980s, which showed that this species had slumped to fewer than 4,000 pairs, there has been a dramatic improvement in barn-owl fortunes. Today the numbers have more than doubled and one major element in that success has been the provision of thousands of nest boxes all over Britain, in which 70 per cent of our population now breeds.

The development of a new kind of nest box specifically suited to the little owl has met with comparable localised success. Fortunately East Anglia is still a little owl stronghold and with the help of a new dedicated Hawk and Owl Trust website (www. littleowlcount.org), to be launched this month, anyone can now log their sightings of the bird. This will provide a clearer picture of where little owls still flourish, but it will also enable the Trust to site the new boxes in areas where they can be most effective. Public information on where the bird breeds will be a critical part of the scheme's success.

Purists may argue that since it was introduced by people this 'foreign' bird should receive no more priority than other undesirable aliens. Technically that position may meet the letter of the law, but the Hawk and Owl Trust argues that it is overly bureaucratic and short-sighted. The owl's arrival has triggered no discernible problem among our native wildlife and now that it has suffered a 40 per cent decline across its entire continental range, the little owl has become a Species of European Conservation Concern. To withhold support from the British population would only heap woe on this delightful and harmless symbol of wisdom.

# DECEMBER

1 December 2015

~ CLAXTON, NORFOLK ~

The wind was bitter and ice-edged and it inflicted a final layer of melancholy on the dank marsh, the slumped reeds, the plain of grey overhead and the River Yare, which was just leaden ooze twisting on an outgoing tide. Eventually I felt it all as the cold ache at my temple.

But other creatures seemed to catch the same mood. Swans in the fields were all gangling necks and heavy waddle, while a buzzard, bulked up with air and feathers as it perched in the copse, flew off with that plodding tempo of its species. Then I climbed the riverbank and suddenly there were the wigeon.

There were 500 spread evenly and receding upstream until they were just pepper spots before a last meander. The current downstream and their foot movements cancelled each other so that the flock looked static. Among the nearest, the colours of the males had a lapidary trueness even in this light: hand-cut lozenges of silica and white marble at the rear, the polished sandstone of their heads, that flake of brightness on the forecrown. They milled and turned, heads up, males and females, and while a flock of teal clattered up and bolted in a globe of fright, the wigeon paused.

All at once near birds peeled upwards, luffing into the breeze, catching all that lift and rising steeply. Wigeon in flight seem so finely engineered, slender winged and pre-oiled so that all parts slide so freely through the air. Birds left. Others returned. Some stayed. But in all that entropy of a wigeon flock in wild motion there was also a sort of warm-blooded joy that even December grey does not extinguish.

Finally they began to call. A wigeon's basic note is a companionable high whistle — *wheee* — with something of the child down a slide. It is contagious, passing to neighbours, until all catch hold and occasionally the notes run together and rise over them as a high-silvered chorus of togetherness and panic. Then they broke through their own sound envelope in a churn of feet, wings and water drops shining like mica: a glittering outburst in a dying season.

## 5 December 2017

### ⤞ ROCKLAND BROAD, NORFOLK ⤝

As the light falls in my neighbouring parish and the mercury drops, so the bird sounds acquire extra layers of intensity. I'm thinking of the hysterical chinking of blackbirds in the ivy and the disembodied sharp *pitt* notes of Cetti's warblers. Most evocative of all, however, are the water rails.

Related to the moorhen and coot, this arch introvert is long-legged and long-billed with a curious laterally compressed body that enables it to thread minuscule gaps between reed stems. It is common in our valley but I seldom see one. Tonight there are four and the way they answer each other's sounds at 100-metre intervals across the marsh tells you everything about their solitariness and oddity.

The quality of water-rail calls is not easy to describe but they create an overarching impression of the owner's tightly wound and distressed condition. This in itself is strange because the bird leads a solitary life buried in deepest cover and the only conclusion one can make is that each water rail dwells in a drama of its making; a character spooked by its own shadow.

The calls include grunts, elongated pig-squeaks or a quiet 'peep' note that is broken and repeated as a pattern of tiny sound granules. Yet out of the erratic repertoire emerges a high, more urgent vocalisation that comes eight or nine times in a falling sequence. It is often described as a squeal but it has a lovely purring quality, particularly as each note dies away.

Norfolk marsh folk found the perfect word for it – to 'sharm' or 'sharming' – presumably after the sound of the shawm, a double-reed woodwind instrument that was popular in the Middle Ages. If you hear a shawm being played you can detect some of the qualities of the water rail's sounds and as I stand in the gloaming by the ice-blue broad I like to think of the word – and the instrument – travelling eastwards through Europe with the returning Crusaders, passing out of the door of the medieval hall, and then trudging out on to the marsh with the Norfolk eel catchers and reedcutters and finally lodging itself as a standard piece of the modern ornithological vocabulary.

## 6 December 2016

### ⊷ Claxton, Norfolk ⊶

I saw the goose skein as a tentative line in a southern blue sky and, since it was arrowed straight towards me, I rested arms and binoculars on a gate to ease the muscle ache.

One then two minutes must have passed as the skein slowly grew, before it occurred to me that large birds in flight never rush. The wing beats are steady, solemn, self-reliant. I remember once in eastern Turkey watching a line of flamingos like this. There is an almost identical length of neck and leg fore and aft of those pink flamingo wings and, such was their lack of progress, it was a good five minutes before I could even work out in which direction they flew.

My guess is that most large species – flamingos, cranes, geese – in their several million years evolving on Earth have not changed, unlike our own species, by so much as a metre per second in pace. Cranes from the Miocene would keep time with cranes today.

It is one of the things to learn from watching birds: to adjust to their timekeeping. In this field I have several heroes. W. H. Hudson once lay for five hours to listen to marsh warblers singing. More impressive was the artist Eric Ennion, who lay in a gun punt, hidden under canvas, for seven hours while drawing black-necked grebes. And for the two whole previous days he had done the same and seen nothing. Only by taking time can one lift aside the common cloth which our senses smother over the daily hours. Only then can we get beneath to the real light-loving fabric of life, whose magic is all here now and nowhere else in that star swarm across the night sky.

My geese arrived: twenty birds in a curve, the lead place switching from the tenth to the fourteenth. They rose and fell, swaying as if one organism were breathing slowly, and as they approached they never made sound above the merest nub of their true music. Once they'd passed overhead, however, out poured the oiled-metal *ank-ang* chorus of pink-footed geese on a north wind.

9 December 2013

CLAXTON, NORFOLK

I should have known when I saw the behaviour of the pheasants, banging repeatedly against the fence, until that small-brained frenzy coincided with a gap, whereupon they rocketed up and away. The perpetual fusillade of guns from across the other side of the Yare sounded like the Somme. One wonders if that audible violence, which is surely peculiar to the killing inflicted by industrial societies, also measures our alienation from the natural landscape. One thinks, by contrast, of the silence and stealth that must always have surrounded hunters from the Paleolithic until the Middle Ages.

Yet this pheasant business probably has more impact on the shape of the British landscape than all the efforts of all the environmental organisations in their entire history. I tried to imagine its key moment – that period at the end of the shoot when the guns walk down the rows of carcasses. Sometimes there are hundreds of birds. The innovation that unleashed this form of arithmetical ritual was the 1847 invention of the breech-loading shotgun. One is tempted to speculate that there is a psychological continuum that stretches from that moment to the high slaughter of modern video games and even perhaps unto Columbine: a view of killing as entertainment with numbers. Yet in real hunting should the hunter not savour death sparingly, ring-fencing it with meaning and significance so that there is a genuine transaction between predator and prey?

When the guns finally fell silent and the countryside was restored to itself I was intrigued to spot a peregrine, whose own prowess probably encompasses a bird catch a day for the whole of its life. This hunter also creates vast commotion in the valley when it is in killing mood. Yet the bird was absolutely silent. It was simply sitting on a post mid field. What was most astonishing was the way that thousands of wildfowl and waders were all around it across the field, quietly feeding while the falcon rested.

## 9 December 2014

### CLAXTON, NORFOLK

At dawn's customary hour (7.30) it was still night and by nine the light looked only just post-dawn. The whole marsh was suffused with a grey so fathomless it felt as if the colour continued in some granular form along the optic nerve to the brain. The mist softened the world's shape, but I noticed as I went through the gate that the full line of willows had finally been rendered down by the last two months of achingly slow mild dullness to the stark bone of twig and branch. All foliage was gone.

How remarkable that even this drab December day just glanced off the goldfinches as if they were made from mercury. The bars of sunflower yellow across the wings sang out, but it was the flight calls that seemed brightest. They have a wind-blown quality, like flakes of gold metal held on threads, dangling and touching in a breeze. Just days earlier I heard the sound on a Barcelonan street, four blocks from the Plaça da Catalunya. It occurred to me then that, had I lived in such a rectilinear canyon of stone, seven floors deep on both sides, I too would keep a caged goldfinch on my balcony.

In the past we were fixated with goldfinch colour. The red around the beak allowed Christian Europe to entwine the bird's story with the Passion. Goldfinches were said to have dipped their faces in Christ's blood as they tried to work those thorns out of his crown. Stranger still was the older Greek myth of the *charadrios*, an unidentified bird whose yellow details were said to work magic on the convalescent. It is this story that accounts for the presence of 486 goldfinches in religious paintings from the late Middle Ages to the Renaissance.

Personally I could forgo those colours, but not that voice. A male bullfinch, with its round breast like a globe of rose pink, yields a song like a tiny globe of softness. Chaffinch song has a cockneyfied rollicking jollity. But goldfinches produce something finer and more invincible, a filigree music grained with joy.

15 December 2015

CLAXTON, NORFOLK

Even as I stepped out, the rain was rattling at the back of my coat. Yet I still needed to release my ears from the noisy tunnel of the hood in order to hear it all the more clearly. Immediately I could pick out a difference between the even fizz of the raindrops on grass and the messier drumbeat under the trees, where the water dripping off branches or twigs created its own counter rhythm to the downpour's wider patter.

Rain blurred the charcoal light of pre-dawn and I had no chance of seeing a robin already in song, nor the wren squeezing out those hard granular alarm notes as I passed. Yet there are fixtures on the marsh that no amount of darkness can hide: the swans' slow upending and the stink of fox by the railway sleepers over the beck. Then there was the crashing away of Chinese water deer – a smudge of roan threading damp reed until it blurred to grey.

The car-park lights at the Beauchamp Arms and the far-off sodium lamps encircling the sugarbeet factory at Cantley gave me a kind of bearing to the Yare. When I finally rose up the bank to get the full glorious wide hiss of the rain on the river, the dawn was coming. To cover the 93 million miles from the sun that light had taken eight minutes. On its near-instantaneous entry into our atmosphere the whole place swelled up in pale calcareous grey light. Woods sprang up, fields rolled flat out and the double line of poplars by the lane were suddenly filled with 2,000 jackdaws from the roost.

I told myself I had come to see them, spread like graphite dust through the arch of tree canopy. I tried to capture exactly an impression of their going as they swarmed off through a tunnel of their own joyous notes. But the words I wrote dissolved into the page even as I scrambled them down and really I sense I had come for dawn itself: the relentlessness of light-loving life that no rain or cloud can brake.

19 December 2017

ROCKLAND ST MARY, NORFOLK

The raised track by the side of this broad is bordered by a dense willow thicket that overtops a network of intertidal creek.

To compensate for its subterranean shadow you have to cowl your eyes and cup your ears to detect any secret occupant. Usually this is little more than a moorhen or roving band of tits, but now and then it is something scarcer like a feeding woodcock. Fixing the whereabouts of these quiet rustlings, which always insert a shudder of excitement, is one's best hope of seeing before being seen.

This time I strained and scanned until the all-seeing gloom hardened into a hunting bird. At the creek edge she was poised with head tilted down and beak angled at the mud like a short spike. Every few seconds, the whole body rose as she raked forward and back then swept her bill sideways like a scythe. The intense, signature practice – for it identified her as a blackbird – simultaneously cleared dripping clouts of muddy moss and leaves but exposed invisible prey that she then darted to pick out with forensic care.

The scene brought to mind those lines from R. S. Thomas ('A Blackbird Singing') that there was 'a suggestion of dark/ Places about it', but also a reflection of how extraordinarily adaptable the species can be. Here it was hunting crake-like, yet for months my Claxton blackbirds have been harvesting fruit: first blackberries, rowan, hawthorn, holly, cotoneaster, pyracantha; now apples and, very soon, ivy.

They are the standard worm catchers on our lawn and even follow our garden mole to profit from his excavations. Yet I remember the feeling of a world subverted when, once, in India, out of the forest darkness, swept a blue whistling thrush with a mouse in its beak like any ravening hawk. British blackbirds too have been noted with this family taste for blood – eel, shrew, newt, fledgling house sparrow, frog, slow worm, snake – and some have even taken to piracy, snatching tiddlers from off a kingfisher's sword-point. Despite all Thomas's suggestions of darkness we should recall that blackbirds can be trained to follow a currant trail right to an out-stretched human hand and on into the kitchen.

## 20 December 2016

>◌ Cʟᴀxᴛᴏɴ, Nᴏʀꜰᴏʟᴋ ◌<

The garden task that gives me greatest satisfaction is the cutting of our winter wood stack. I like to joke that our logburner consumes only hand-prepared organic 'food', and there is even a sense in which each piece is an individual.

Over the years I've learnt that the secret to preparing logs is not some fancy axe or equipment: it is time. I have thus worked out a four-stage process that spans two years, beginning with the moment when the live trees are felled.

They are mainly self-sown sallows that sprang up just after the war on the edge of my four boundary dykes at Blackwater Carr, when the fen was open grazing marsh. Decades of non-intervention allowed them to develop into linear thickets the length of the whole site. Rather than permitting the mature trees to choke the dykes with leaf mulch I clear them off the banks while simultaneously restoring the original flower-rich pasture.

Before the fresh timber is transported it forms an initial stack at Blackwater. The first six to ten months of seasoning, completed under tarpaulin, allows it to be used by breeding solitary wasps or by overwintering ruby tiger moth caterpillars. Then comes a second rest after its transfer to Claxton, where it creates another great invertebrate habitat, especially for woodlouse spiders and a lovely group of moths called flatbodies.

Finally comes the log splitting for the woodsheds, when they are cut and restacked for anything up to six months in advance of use. In his book *Wildwood*, Roger Deakin suggested that he was warmed three times by his logs: when they were felled, while being split and then finally as they burned.

I enjoy an imaginative corollary, savouring each piece when I try to recall the circumstances of its felling, how it was subsequently stored and then the moment it was sectioned to fit the fire. By the time it goes through the glass door I have two years of connection and something about many pieces – the

girth of the trunk, details in its bark, the way it split or patterns
in the grain – permits me to recognise them in their slow journey
to the flames.


## 23 December 2013

### ⤞ BLACKWATER CARR, NORFOLK ⤝

There are precious few instances when modern farming seems
at peace with nature, but this moment by the beet field under
the winter sun was glorious. The constituent parts were entirely
prosaic. There was a huge bright-red harvester going back and
forth along the beet rows. This machine aligned its operations
with a John Deere tractor and trailer that intermittently
dumped the beet on an ever-larger sugar mountain by the field
edge.

Enveloping all the agricultural action was a ceaseless flow
of about 500 black-headed gulls. Bird for bird, this species is a
modest beast. In winter the creature looks glinting white against
the dank land, but in detail its pearl-grey wings bear a pale blade
on the leading edge and each fan is obliquely angled at its mid
point like a scimitar. In concert these wings create an aura of
flashing motion around the bird's pink bill and dangled red legs.
In unison a flock of 500 produced a shining river of movement
that washed over and crazed the sculptural outline of man's
machines in watery lines of grey and silver.

Together the birds and humans enfolded their shared action
in audible dissonance. The grind of gears and engine noise and
then all that vile swede-sour sweetness tumbling heavily on to the
steel plate of the trailer floor all cut across the wild music of the
birds' rolling 'craa' notes. Yet the entire vision itself seemed nicely
unified. There was even a distinct visual rhyme between the
perpetual wheel of the birds and the toothed belt that relentlessly
dug the beet out of the soil, then uplifted the crop to a holding
bin on the harvester's back.

Adorning the scene were a few filigree details: a scatter of pied wagtails that swirled up and around the larger event in airy lines, a marsh harrier twisting overhead against the burning sun, and then the surrounding stoical bare dark oaks that turned a field into a moment of English theatre.

## 23 December 2014

### ❦ CLAXTON, NORFOLK ❦

I inched forward and was suddenly eyeball to eyeball with what is surely one of the sweetest faces in all British nature. A Chinese water deer has dark liquid eyes emphasised by a ring of pale around each socket. Even its shortsightedness adds a layer of endearment. When quiet and unaware of human presence the beast has a rather comedic bustling manner. Once it is alarmed, the round teddy bear's ears bat back and forth like radar discs, while a wet button nose jabs skywards as it samples the alien presence its vision cannot quite resolve. When a deep draught of danger finally hits the brain, the creature turns and loops away, thrusting a big bottom up and down in undulating flight. If really spooked at close quarters the deer assumes an enormous head-down drive in its forward run.

When caught full-face at leisure, however, a male Chinese water deer also has a little of the demonic image that environmentalists frequently project on to non-native species. Curving down from his upper jaw are two fangs that bury their sharp tips in pale fur at his throat side. Vampire he may look, but I was intrigued to hear how, according to one Norfolk estate manager, the species was having no detectable detrimental impact on the farm or the native flora and fauna. Unlike other deer (or rabbits and hares), this species doesn't take bark off trees or nibble saplings, nor does it eat arable crops. In fact, of all alien species the Chinese water deer may have more moral claim to protection in this country than any other.

In China it's now thought to number as few as 10,000 because of habitat loss and persecution (the semi-digested milk in the fawn's stomach has an assumed medicinal value). This shrinkage in the home contingent means that our population assumes an ever-increasing importance in the species' survival. Contrary to its fortunes in Asia, the deer here has gone from 600 in 1994 to 1,500 in 2004. My sense is that over the decade the trend has strongly continued, especially in the Norfolk Broads.

## 29 December 2015

### ⟨⟨ CLAXTON, NORFOLK ⟩⟩

Anyone who ever put in a hard stint of gardening knows the moment. The tasks are at a natural end. The tools are all stowed. There is even a satisfying link between your heavy limbs and the sense of rough order pulled out of the hedge and lawn and gathered up in the fresh-edged wood stack. The loss of light, the swelling damp and the quietness of the air after all the brisk morning – even the day and season seem to join in this aura of things completed.

You pause to enjoy all of it. And in a corner, where the holly breaks the last dim daylight, there is a wandering smoke billow of tiny insects. There are no more than a score but you wonder have these flies emerged just, or have you acquired the peace of mind to see them only now? And rather like the garden's pleasing order, are they a gift only of hard work?

This silence-spiralling formation has a wonderful name – a 'ghost' – while the creatures themselves have a technical label. They are in the family *Trichoceridae*, and are related to crane flies, although they lack the daddy-long-legs' extravagance of limb. They are smaller and while they are commonplace in autumn and spring, it is this emergence now that gives them a common name. Winter gnats. They will ghost even with snow on the ground.

The immatures feed upon plant decay so this brief vapour of flying adults is really leaf litter made into a dance. It coils through the gloom and offers a final thought. Winter gnats belong to an order that is central to all biodiversity: the flies. They may include disease carriers, bloodsuckers and crop destroyers but flies number more than 7,000 species in Britain (that exceeds all the varieties of bird in Africa and South America). Worldwide there are 150,000 named forms, which is at least one-tenth of all recognised species. Collectively flies and their like drive the natural order of life. In transmuted form they are the salmon's leap, the otter's splash and the sparrowhawk's dive but also the song thrush song from our holly tops once April comes.

# INDEX